ADVENTURES
of a
CODA

Child of Deaf Adults

RUTH A. REPPERT

PRESS

Adventures of a CODA
Child of Deaf Adults
by Ruth A. Reppert

Cover Photo: The Author at Two

Printed in the United States of America.

ISBN 9781498461665

www.xulonpress.com

ACKNOWLEDGEMENTS

Cover Design: Peter J. Thorpe

Drawings: Linda Reppert Gritta

Editing: Thomas McCauley and Neil Starr

In loving memory of my parents

Edwin M. Hazel and Irene S. Hazel 1931

"The behavior of every individual is a product of his environmental experience."

Maria Montessori
The Absorbent Mind

CONTENTS

ILLUSTRATIONS

PROVISO

I n this writing, I use the terms "sign language" and "signing" as we did in my era; they include any manner of signed communication used within the Deaf community. Around 1965, the term "American Sign Language" (ASL) appeared, and it identifies a type of signing having its own distinctive grammar, unrelated to English, and the characteristics of a true language.

I have lived in two cultures, the "Deaf World" and the "Hearing World," and, to emphasize those two cultures, I capitalize the words, "Deaf" and "Hearing." When the word "deaf" appears without capitalization, it refers to the physical condition.

Just as my two worlds differ in their languages, this writing differentiates sign language with *italics* but presents it in English as a sign language interpreter might express it. While the conversations may not be exact, I have kept their original meaning.

Within these pages, I share some of my personal experiences as I remember them. The scenes begin over eighty years ago, the earliest ones rooted in stories told and retold by my parents and relatives.

I invite you to travel along with me as I relive my unusual life adventures. This journey may forever expand your worldview. It did so for me!

Ruth A. Reppert

THE SETTING

It's 1933, the period of the Great Depression. The stock market has crashed, thousands of banks are closed, unemployment is widespread, food is scarce, and the poor stand in long lines outside of soup kitchens. Each person who qualifies receives a booklet of food stamps to purchase food.

The National Association of the Deaf (NAD) is defending the right of the deaf to drive a vehicle and is calling for the end to discrimination in hiring and employment practices.

Edwin and Irene Hazel are Deaf. Ed lost his job, his house, and his savings, and he is now suffering from stomach ulcers, too ill to work. To pay the bills, Irene got a full-time job in the laundry of the nearby Western Pennsylvania School for the Deaf, a residential school for deaf children. It is the school that Irene attended through high school.

I was born to the Hazels during these hard times.

A Hearing child of Deaf adults, I was destined to live an extraordinary life.

PROLOGUE

C lick! Click! Click! I hear the cleats on my favorite uncle's shoes drumming the cement as he walks toward us. Dropping my dolly, I eagerly toddle toward the back door. My Uncle Dan is coming! When Daddy sees me going in that direction, he rises from his chair and strides past me, throwing the door open wide to the tune of rusty hinges.

The bright morning sunlight blinds me for an instant as it rushes into the kitchen, framing Uncle Dan's silhouette as he towers above us. Greeting Daddy with a handshake and a nod, he reaches for me. "Hello, princess," he exclaims as he sweeps me high above his head. I'm hanging in space, squealing with delight as the sight of the floor far below takes my breath away. My uncle draws me close to his shoulder, takes my lunch bag from Dad, turns, and starts walking. He's taking me to Gramma's before he goes to work.

I eagerly look forward to the next part of our trip. Resting my chin on his shoulder, I search the ground behind him. Yes! There are the backs of his shoes, first one and then the other, while the cleats tap in rhythm with each step. I am staring and listening, spellbound.

"Here we are, honey, we're going down. One, two, three, ..." Uncle Dan counts the steps aloud as we descend the cement stairway down the steep hillside, through the trees and brush, to Frankstown Avenue.

Reaching the bottom, we cross the busy street and walk through a dark narrow alleyway that leads to the row houses on Conemaugh Street. "We're going to Gramma's, we're going to Gramma's," he chants in familiar singsong. Soon I hear, "Cumma to Gramma," and I turn to see Gramma's arms open wide for me. But, before Uncle Dan gives me to her, he looks closely into my eyes.

"Ruth Ann, listen carefully. You are too young to understand, but try to remember this."

"God knew what He was doing when He sent you to your mommy and daddy. They will need you."

Uncle Dan's words are forever in my memory.

The Stairway to Frankstown Avenue

I

EMBARKING
1933-1945

"When I was a child, I talked like a child,
I thought like a child, I reasoned like a child."

1 Corinthians 11a, NET

Chapter I

INITIATION

Edwin M. Hazel paces the waiting room of Pittsburgh's Mercy Hospital, pausing at the window to watch the swirling leaves at the lighted entrance. It has been a long day, and it's almost midnight. Why hasn't Dr. West appeared? Troubled and tired, Edwin sits down beside his mother-in-law and her daughter.

Soon Dr. West, dressed in scrubs, enters the room and walks to Edwin. "Congratulations!" the doctor says loudly, "You have a baby girl." The words, heard by others in the room, fall on deaf ears.

Edwin offers a pen and notepad, and the doctor hastily scrawls his announcement, handing them back. Edwin writes another note: "How is my wife?"

With a tired sigh, Dr. West hastily scribbles, "Fine," and they repeat the exchange. Abruptly abandoning his efforts, the doctor turns his attention to the women sitting beside the new father.

Alone in his silence, Edwin ponders the exciting news: Irene is fine, and our daughter, Ruth Ann, is here, "Ruth" for my mother, and "Ann" for Irene's mother. He practices forming his baby daughter's name on his lips.

Meanwhile, Dr. West notes that one of the women appears to be an immigrant: white hair fashioned in a bun, freshly-ironed cotton housedress, and gold hoop earrings. The other is a girl about twelve whose features suggest Italian heritage. He greets them. "Hello, I'm Dr. West. Are you related to Mrs. Hazel?"

The girl replies for her mother. "Yes, I'm Toni, Irene's sister, and this is our mother, Anna Schifino."

"Well, congratulations upon the arrival of a new granddaughter and a new niece," he says. "Err... umm...May I ask?...How can the Hazels care for their child if they can't hear her cries?"

Again, Toni replies, "My sister and brother-in-law have their ways, and they plan to keep the baby at their house. We live nearby to help them."

"Good!" says Dr. West, "that settles my concern." He presses further. "I'm curious about something else, too. Mrs. Hazel and I converse easily by speaking, but Mr. Hazel and I can't understand each other unless we write notes. Why is there such a difference?"

"That's easy," says Toni. "Irene could hear and speak until she was ten when spinal meningitis left her deaf. That's why she speaks well and reads lips. But Edwin lost most of his hearing from ear infections as a baby. He never heard words spoken, so he has trouble pronouncing them. Most people can't understand him when he speaks, and that's why he writes notes. But I understand him, and I can fingerspell words, too."

"Good for you," says the doctor, "and thanks for the explanation. Since her parents were not born deaf, this child probably can hear."

He draws closer to them and lowers his voice. "Mrs. Hazel had a long hard labor, so we delivered the baby by Caesarean section. Please tell Mr. Hazel that, because his wife is a charity case, her hospital stay must be shortened. He is to take his wife and baby home on Wednesday." Toni says, "I will tell him," and Dr. West bids them goodbye, quickly walks past the new father, and leaves the room.

Edwin, awakened from his reverie, eagerly asks Toni, "What did the doctor say?" She falters and then fingerspells, *"l-a-t-e-r."*

Sighing with resignation, Edwin leads the way out of the room, and the three head for the parking lot and his 1928 Model A Ford...

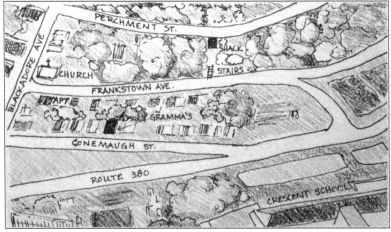

My Neighborhood

Wednesday morning dawns, and Daddy is happily driving Mommy and me home. "Up we go on Blackadore Avenue and Perchment Street hills," Daddy says gaily, and, parking in front of a little shack, he announces, "We're home!" "Home" is a rickety little hovel that hangs on the side of a steep hill. It has a living room, a bedroom, and a bathroom on the street level, and a kitchen and basement on the same lower level.

Daddy switches the engine off and signs to Mommy, *"Wait here while I take the baby inside."* He picks me up and carries me in the front door, through the small living room, and into the tiny bedroom. Gingerly, he lays me in the big crib that is wedged beside Mommy's side of their bed. Then, Daddy returns to the car, helps Mommy inside, and eases her into bed.

She signs, *"I will sleep with one arm through the crib slats, and, if I feel her crying or restless, I will tend to her."* Daddy interrupts. *"For now, that is not necessary, you must rest. I will care for her, and, if I need your help, I will tap you awake."*

Mommy nods her agreement and then frets. *"Do we have enough milk for the baby?"* "Yes," Daddy replies, *"we have plenty of milk. I used the extra food stamps the doctor approved. My ulcers must wait."*

Mommy worries, *"I must get back to work at the laundry soon, or I might lose my job. Are you sure you can manage?"* Daddy smiles. *"Ruth Ann and I will get along fine. When I am better, I will accept that night job I was offered, and your mother and sisters will take care of her during the day."* With her concerns now quieted, Mommy closes her eyes in exhaustion.

Now Daddy speaks to me. "Hello, Ruth Ann! I will try hard to talk so you will understand me, and I will teach you some signs, too." Soon I am screaming in hunger. Daddy shows my bottle to me, pops the nipple into my eager mouth and says, "milk," signing the word at the same time.

My eyes are wide as I watch his sign, and I am alert as I listen to his soft voice, soothing to my ears...

The Shack and the 1928 Model A Ford

Eighteen months pass quickly, and I am thriving on Daddy's daily loving care. He sometimes speaks and sometimes signs to me, and I'm beginning to understand him. When Mommy is home, she signs and speaks English to me at the same time. So here I am, learning to fit into the Hearing World and the Deaf World as best I can.

I have already developed a sense of my parents' disability and how to deal with it. I often see my parents calling each other by stomping on the wooden floor or by waving to attract each other's attention. So, when a knock sounds at our door, I bang on my high chair tray to get their notice. It works!

I don't realize it, but the thump causes a vibration to travel down the wooden legs of my chair and across the wood flooring to the soles of their feet.

When they turn to me, I look at the door and wave at it. Every time this happens, Daddy declares with a chuckle, "Ruth Ann, you are no dumbbell, you are our doorbell," and he always gives me a hug...

For two years, now, Mommy has been teaching me, and, tonight, she taught me to sign another sentence: "*I love Mommy and Daddy.*" I watch her pick up her "Baby's Record Book," open it, and write my latest accomplishment, adding it to a long list. Speaking and signing to me at the same time, she says, "You are a smart girl, Ruth Ann. You can make more than fifty signs, and you can form the Manual Alphabet on your fingers when I name the A-B-Cs. Someday you will use them to fingerspell words."

After breakfast, Daddy sets me on his lap. "Ruth Ann," he says, "Mother told me you know many signs, and I am proud of you. I think you are smart enough to learn a new game, so watch me carefully. He signs, "*You hide somewhere in the house, and I will look for you. If I find you, I win. But, if I can't find you, you win. Understand?*" I nod yes. "*O-K, go hide*

22

now," he says, and, scurrying to find a hiding place, I stand behind the bathroom door and close my eyes.

"Where is Ruth Ann? Where is Ruth Ann?" Daddy chants, pretending to look downstairs and upstairs. I hear him pass my hiding place, and, just when I think I've won, he grabs me. "Ha, ha, you can't fool me," he cries, and, scooping me up, he tickles me mercilessly while I squeal with delight. *"Again, again,"* I sign, and I'm off to find a new hiding place.

After lunch, Daddy puts me down for a nap. Soon the silence is broken by a funny sound that wakens me. I climb out of my crib and follow it to the living room, and there is Daddy, sitting in his favorite chair with his eyes closed, and that funny sound is coming from his mouth.

As I slowly draw closer, he opens his eyes and cries, "BOO!" and we laugh at my startle. "I love you SO much," he declares, his arms open wide for a hug. *"I love you, too,"* I sign...

Daddy entertains me with games, but, since I've turned three, our routine has changed because he has a job. He works at night and sleeps during the day, and that means I must spend weekdays at Gramma's house. Mommy says it is my nursery school.

Gramma's row house has four rooms: a living room and kitchen on the first floor, two small bedrooms upstairs, and a toilet in the cellar where the "shower" consists of a shower head fastened to a ceiling water pipe and suspended above the floor drain.

The fenced back yard is a section of paved concrete about twelve feet square, with five cement steps that lead up to the back door.

The attached houses are identical and located on Conemaugh Street where Italian immigrant families and "colored people," as Gramma calls them, live in harmony. My grandfather works for the city as a landscape gardener and seldom is home. That's why I call it "Gramma's house."

Unlike my quiet home, this house is often filled with noisy activity, and I am fascinated by the family interactions, squabbles, and sibling rivalries. I'm learning how Hearing people live and speak...

I've spent the daytime hours this week at Gramma's, and it is Sunday night. Mommy, Daddy, and I just returned from an all-day picnic with Deaf friends. Mommy bathed me and lingers in the bathroom while Daddy leads me to my crib, now beside the bathroom door near his side of the bed.

After he tucks me in, he signs emphatically to me. *"Pay attention! DO NOT climb out of your crib tonight. When you turn the light on, you wake us up."* And, shaking his finger in my face, he continues. *"If you climb out, I will give you a spanking."* His hands mimic the promised blows in mid-air. I dutifully nod yes and sign, *"promise."* As I settle down to sleep. I hear Mommy come into the room, turn off the ceiling light, and climb into bed.

Soon I'm wakened by her pleading voice:"Ruth Ann, please bring me a glass of water." I bolt upright and peer through the darkness, my body frozen in fear, my thoughts whirling. Daddy said I must NOT get out of my crib. Maybe, if I wait, Mommy will fall asleep and forget the water. I clench the crib bars, listening.

Her voice pierces the silence. "Ruth Ann, if you don't bring me a glass of water, I will spank you." I scramble to my feet and grasp the crib rail. What shall I do? Daddy has never spanked me, but Mommy does spank, so I know for certain that she will smack me if I disobey her.

Anxiously, I climb out of my crib, walk into the bathroom, and, on tiptoe, I turn on the light. Before I can reach for the glass, Daddy's two powerful hands lift me from behind and firmly carry me to the big bed. By the light streaming from the bathroom, he plops me face-down across his lap and begins to spank me.

I am screaming and kicking when light from the ceiling floods the room, and Daddy's blows come to a sudden halt. Through my tears, I glimpse Mommy signing to Daddy in amazement, *"WHAT ARE YOU DOING?"* They are signing to each other as I wail.

Daddy sets me on his lap and signs, *"I'm sorry I spanked you, Ruth Ann, it was a mistake,"* and Mommy adds, "I didn't see Daddy sign his orders to you." She gets a drink and returns to bed while Daddy wipes my tears and walks me to my crib. After giving me a hug, he tucks me in, turns off the light, and goes to bed. Tomorrow will be a workday for both of them.

I cry in the darkness, struggling to understand their words, but all I can think is my daddy spanked me. I hurt deep inside, and I feel my first sting of injustice as my sobs usher me into troubled slumber.

The dawn wakens me, and last night's incident has faded from memory. Although I don't understand the concept of forgiveness, I greet Daddy with a smile. I am unaware that last night's event is a preview of the distressing experiences yet to come...

We're in the kitchen today when I run to Daddy and tap him, and he looks at me questioningly. I point and sign, *"I hear a funny sound in there."* He walks into the basement and comes back with a mouse in a trap. I watch him with curiosity.

"This is a mouse trap, and this is how it works. When a mouse tries to eat the cheese, this bar snaps and catches him. Then I take the mouse to the field and let him go. We don't want mice in the house because they eat our food."

The bar is holding the mouse's tail, so the little animal is uninjured. *"Can I keep him?"* I sign to Daddy.

Mommy sees our conversation and protests, signing and speaking at the same time. "Mice are dirty animals, and they sometimes bite. I don't think they make good pets."

But I jump up and down, signing, *"please, please, please,"* so, over Mommy's objection, Daddy says, *"O-K, Ruth Ann, you can keep this mouse for a pet."* I triumphantly sign, *"Thank you."*

Mommy's face shows she is not happy with his answer, but, after she and Daddy sign to each other for a while, she stops objecting and says cheerily with a smile, "Have a nice stroll," and she winks at Daddy. I wonder what that wink means, but I'm puzzled just for a moment.

Daddy uses a string as a leash, tying one end of it around the mouse's neck and the other end around my wrist. My little pet is pulling hard; he wants to get started. "Come, let's take your pet for a walk," Daddy says with a twinkle in his eye, so out the back door we go, down the cement steps to Frankstown Avenue. Daddy holds my hand as we cross the street, and, when we reach the sidewalk on the other side, we start walking down Frankstown Avenue with my little pet scampering in the lead.

A man stops to speak to me. "I like your little pet," he says. I sign his comment to Daddy who smiles and nods to him. We take a few more steps, and a lady stops and says, "Oh what a cute little mouse." I sign this to Daddy, and he nods to her. Then she asks me, "What is your mouse's name?" I sign this to Daddy, my face questioning. He smiles and says, *"YOU think of a name, Ruth Ann,"* so I think. Then I tell the lady, "My pet's name is Mr. Mouse."

Daddy asks me, *"What is the name you told her?"*

I don't know how to make the name with my fingers, so I reply, *"I will tell Mommy the name when we get home, and she will spell it for you."*

Daddy smiles and says, *"Good idea."*

After being stopped by several more walkers, we arrive at a big house. Daddy opens the front door and takes me inside, saying, "Let's show your pet to our dentist. He is the man who takes care of our teeth, and I want you to meet him." We are the only ones waiting here in this room when a colored man wearing a short white coat appears. Smiling his welcome, he shakes Daddy's hand.

The dentist reads Daddy's notepad and looks down at me. "Hello, Ruth Ann," he says, "I am Dr. Avent. What a cute little pet you have. What's his name?" I proudly say, "His name is Mr. Mouse." "Nice name," Dr. Avent says, "and I'm glad you brought him to show me.

While you are here, your father wants me to look at your teeth. I take care of your mom and dad's teeth, too. So, every time you visit me, I will give you a ride in my special chair and clean your teeth. Would you like a ride now?" I nod yes.

After Daddy unties Mr. Mouse and takes the string, Dr. Avent gives me a chair ride. I squeal with delight as he rocks me back and forth and ends my ride by rubbing my teeth with a tool that buzzes.

"You have pretty teeth, Ruth Ann, and I will keep them looking nice," he says, "but you must help take care of them, too. Here is your very own toothbrush, use it every day," and he gives me a little paper bag.

I say "Thank you," as Daddy reties Mr. Mouse to my wrist and thanks Dr. Avent with a knowing nod and a smile. As we leave, I wave goodbye to our dentist, and, peeking into the bag, I discover a tiny doll and a toothbrush with a Mickey Mouse head. I am thrilled!

Walking toward home, I sign to Daddy, *"He is a nice man, and I like him. When can we visit him again?"* Daddy smiles and replies, "Soon."

We climb up the cement steps to our back door, and, once we are in the kitchen, Daddy unties the string around my wrist so I can go upstairs to the bathroom. When I return, I don't see Daddy or Mr. Mouse. In alarm, I ask Mommy, "Where are Daddy and Mr. Mouse?" She looks sad as she replies, "The mouse got loose and ran away, and Daddy is trying to find him."

Daddy appears and announces that he didn't find Mr. Mouse, and he calmly reassures me there will probably be another mouse in the trap soon. With that settled, I turn to tell Mommy about our visit to Dr. Avent. Then, opening my paper bag, I proudly show her my pretty little dolly and my brand new Mickey Mouse toothbrush...

It's Saturday, and Daddy is working overtime. After breakfast, I trail Mommy into the basement. She is sorting the laundry at one end while I am exploring at the opposite end. When I hear her walking back to the kitchen, I run to follow, but, before I can reach her, she walks into the kitchen and locks the door behind her. Click! Frantically, I try to turn the knob, but it won't budge. I'm trapped! No one knows I'm in here!

Fear and panic grip me, and I scream as I pound on the door as hard as I can, yelling, "Help! Help! You locked me in." I listen, and I hear Mommy's footsteps as she walks up the stairs to the living room and then through the bedroom. She is calling me. "Ruth Ann, Ruth Ann, where are you?" and I shout in answer, "I'm here!" But Mommy doesn't come. My cries choke me, and I'm filled with terror as tears come rushing in torrents down my cheeks. I must do something. I must rescue myself.

Through a blur of tears, I see a big box under the high basement window and desperately scramble up on it. The window is open, so I stand on tiptoe to get close to the opening, and I yell toward it. Maybe our next door neighbor will hear me. Over and over I shout until my voice is hoarse. "Florence! Help! Help!" Finally, pausing for a breath, I hear voices in the kitchen. Yes! It's Florence, and she is telling Mommy I'm in here. With a sob of relief, I climb down carefully and run to the door just as Mommy is unlocking it. When she pushes it open, I throw myself into her arms.

I am trembling and sobbing, so Mommy hugs me tight and softly wipes my tears away as she carries me to the kitchen table. She sets me down gently, gives me a drink of water, and waits for me to stop crying.

Tipping my chin, she looks closely into my eyes and says, "Listen carefully, Ruth Ann. I didn't see you follow me into the basement, so I didn't know you were in there with me. I thought you were playing a hiding game somewhere in the house. I can't hear your voice or your footsteps, so you must be sure that I see you. Then this won't happen again."

Gazing into her eyes, a startling thought suddenly enters my mind, and it jolts me.

It's MY fault that Mommy locked me in the basement!

Ruth Ann at Three

Uncle Dan delivers me to Gramma, and she carries me into her tiny living room, latching the screen door behind her. "I'ma locka da screena so nobody, he willa come in when I'ma no see," she says.

We follow the aroma of tomatoes and spices into the small kitchen, and Gramma sets me in a chair at the table so I can watch her.

"I'ma mayka ravioli fora Sunday. I'ma cooka da sauce now. Awla my kids—Nick, Irene, Andy, Dan, Lena,

Mary, Millie, Toni—an awla bambinos cummun da eat every Sunday."

She thrusts her fork as she says each name, crimping the edges of little cheese-filled pillows made of homemade pasta. A "beep, beep" from the street interrupts her. "It'sa da chickena man!" Gramma exclaims, and she sets the fork down, wipes her hands on her apron, and rushes toward the front door.

I slide off the chair and scamper after her, for I am like Gramma's shadow, following her everywhere and watching her every activity. "You stay righta there," she orders firmly as she opens the screen door, letting it slam shut behind her, so I stay inside and watch through the screen.

A rusty old truck is parked at the curb, its bed filled with cages of cackling chickens. I watch as Gramma pokes her hand into one cage after another, methodically feeling each chicken.

She comes back carrying two fat ones. "I'ma fixa deez fera supa," she explains, and, latching the screen door behind her, she carries her prizes through the kitchen and to the cellar as I follow her down the steps. At the bottom, I stop just outside of Grampap's wine cellar. I won't get any closer to Gramma now because I'm not sure of what will happen.

Gramma has hardly begun the process when I cry out in horror, "Gramma! Stop!" and I scramble up the steps, cringing as I hear the flapping of wings. Gramma hurries upstairs to reassure me. "It'sa OK. Chickens giv ussa meat fora food," and, setting me back on the chair, she says, "Letsa finish mayka da ravioli," and she picks up her fork and continues forming crimps.

Aunt Millie comes downstairs, walks straight to Gramma, and bends close to her ear. I can barely hear my aunt's voice. "Why did you let her go down there with you?" Aunt Millie is frowning, and she sounds like she is scolding. Gramma doesn't answer.

Then, Aunt Millie turns to me, and, with a cheery voice and a smile, she says, "Good morning, Ruth Ann, how's my girl today?" She picks me up and carries me into the living room. As we plop into the overstuffed chair, she says brightly, "Let's have some story time," and I clap with delight. I feel safe and loved when I sit in Aunt Millie's lap. She is like a mother to me when Mommy is at work.

Snuggling down to her warmth and her flowery fragrance, I look at the picture book open in front of her. On this page, there is a man with a tall fluffy white hat, and he is holding a cake pan. I listen as Aunt Millie reads in cadence:

> "Pat-a-cake, pat-a-cake, baker's man,
> Make a cake as fast as you can.
> Pat it, and roll it, and mark it with a 'B,'
> And put it in the oven for baby and me."

As she recites the words, she moves my hands to mimic the actions: making cake dough, patting it, rolling it, marking it, opening the oven, and sliding the cake inside. I giggle with enchantment. "More, more," I plead, so she gladly turns the page to another nursery rhyme. Times like these are a treat, for they rarely happen at home.

But the magic of the moment is interrupted by Gramma who has finished her food preparation and is carrying a basket of wet laundry. "You wanna cumma helpa me, Ruth Ann?" she asks. In reply, I slide off Aunt Millie's lap and eagerly follow Gramma out the front door, across Conemaugh Street, and to the big field. I have my regular job to do.

I have seen Gramma gather weeds growing in this field and cook them for dinner, but, today she is hanging clothes on a line someone has put up. "You giva me da cloza pins," she directs. I feel grown up as I put the wooden clothespins into her outstretched hand, one by one, until all the clothes are swinging in the breeze. When the job is finished, back inside we go. Oh! Aunt Mary is here to eat lunch! She must have come in the back door.

Gramma clears the table and calls, "Luncha time," and she sets out the Italian bread, antipasto, pasta fagioli, glasses for wine, and a plate for each person—except for me. I don't need a plate because I have the bag lunch Mommy made and the glass of milk Gramma poured for me.

Everyone is talking and laughing as they eat, and I am unpacking my lunch when, all of a sudden, they stop talking, and it's strangely quiet. I look up to see Grampap entering the back door. Without a word, he pulls a chair to the table and sits down beside me. Gramma rushes to fix his plate, and I notice her hand trembling as she pours his wine, but I am untroubled by her flurry. I open my lunch bag, set my big shiny red apple on my napkin, and start to eat my sandwich. Silence like this is unusual at Gramma's. At home, I'm used to the sound of my own munching and the clacking of knives and forks breaking the silence, but never here. I'm puzzled.

Without warning, Grampap reaches over and grabs my apple. "Grampap," I protest loudly, "that is my apple, give it back." I think maybe he is teasing me like Daddy sometimes does, but, to my horror, Grampap bites into my apple and is chomping it as I watch him in shock and disbelief. I am feeling the familiar sting of injustice.

Gramma hurries to soothe me with a small apple from the icebox, and, with a hug, she assures me, "Dohna be mad ata Grampap, he luvsa you."

Bewildered by her words, I search Grampap's face, and his eerie grin frightens me. My tummy is in a knot, and I barely finish my lunch. I definitely will not touch Gramma's apple, and I'm determined to keep away from Grampap whenever I possibly can.

After a fitful nap, I climb downstairs from the bedroom and see Aunt Toni. Home from high school, she beckons, "Come sit on my lap, honey, I'm painting my fingernails." I watch closely: dip the brush, dab the nail, and see the pink color. "Me too?" I ask, and she colors my nails. "Blow," she says, "it will dry the polish." As we blow, my upset with Grampap and with his nasty behavior subsides, temporarily.

When we finish, she says, "Let's go outside and swing," and, helping me off her lap, she leads the way to the porch as I follow. We are swinging higher and higher, back and forth, as the chains that hold the swing serenade us with their "creak, creak," and we merrily chant to the rhythm of the swinging.

"See, saw, marjory daw,
Jack shall have a new master.
He shall have but a penny a day
Because he can't work any faster."

I hear Mommy's voice at the back door, and she is talking with Aunt Millie and Gramma, but I won't go to them today. I'd rather stay here with Aunt Toni.

Soon Mommy comes out on the porch. "It's time to come home with me, Ruth Ann." I keep swinging, and I shake my head no. Snuggling up to Aunt Toni, I scowl and sign, *"I don't want to go home, I want to stay here,"* and I plead, *"please, please,"* as my tears begin.

Aunt Toni stops the swing and gently nudges me toward Mommy. "Don't cry, Ruth Ann, you must go home now, but, tomorrow, Uncle Dan will bring you back here." And Mommy says brightly, "Yes, Aunt Toni is right, you will come here to Gramma's tomorrow." And, over my protests, Mommy scoops me up and carries me out the door as I look back longingly at Aunt Toni, my eyes brimming with tears.

We arrive home, and Mommy is preparing supper at the stove while I sit on the steps, pouting and staring at my puzzle blocks. I feel sorry for myself. Suddenly,

I jump up, run to her, and tug at her apron. Mommy pauses her work to glance at me over her shoulder. *"Come play with me,"* I plead, but she answers in a dismissive way: "I can't, I'm busy."

With that reply, my frustration explodes. Stomping my foot, I shout and sign, *"Busy, busy, busy! You never have time for me."* Mommy looks at me in surprise and then, without a word, turns back to the stove. Feeling rejected and discouraged, I return to the steps, grumbling to myself. Mommy is always busy. I wish I had a sister to play with me.

At bedtime, Mommy finishes bathing me and asks, "Did you have fun at Gramma's today?" I nod yes, but I'm still feeling gloomy. My face must show it because, when she is tucking me in bed, she rephrases her question: "What happened today at Gramma's?" Reliving the moments, I complain as more anger tumbles out. "Gramma hurt the poor little chickens. They were flapping, and blood was spilling on the floor. I don't ever want to eat chicken again!" Mommy calmly says, "Gramma is sorry she let you watch, it won't happen again. Someday you may change your mind, but, for now, don't worry, we won't make you eat any chicken."

"And Grampap ate my apple!" I blurt out. "Gramma told me about that, too," she says. "What he did doesn't seem fair, but it's just his way of teasing you. Someday you will understand. Meanwhile, here's an idea," she adds. "If Grampap sits beside you during lunch again, why don't you leave your apple in your lunchbag until you've finished eating your sandwich? Then, take the apple out and eat it before Grampap sees it."

I've never thought of that! Excitedly, I nod yes and reply, *"I will."* I'm calmer now that I know what I will do if Grampap sits beside me at the table again.

"Goodnight," Mommy says, "don't worry because tomorrow will be a better day." She turns off the light and closes the door. In the darkness, I listen to the tap of her feet descending the stairs to the kitchen, and I hear paper bags crinkle as she packs lunches. I stare into the black void, aching for a hug, but Mommy never hugs and kisses like Daddy does. Nevertheless, I know she loves me, for she buys me pretty clothes, cooks yummy food, and always serves us homemade cake with a scoop of ice cream for dessert.

Today's events now crowd my mind. I do have fun at Gramma's noisy house, but I like our quiet house, too. Here I can think about what happened during the day and talk with Mommy or Daddy about it. They help me understand. Comforted by these latest thoughts, the frustrations of my day fade away, and I drift into a peaceful sleep...

It's Sunday already, and Daddy, Mommy, and I have arrived at Gramma's. As usual, everyone is crowding around the kitchen table, helping themselves to the delicious food that Gramma has prepared. One by one, we carry our plates to the living room or to the porch and sit down to eat from plates balanced on our laps.

There are seven aunts and uncles, and they greet us warmly. I sign what they say—always for Daddy and sometimes for Mommy—but my cousins avoid my parents. I think it might be because my cousins don't know how to talk to them.

My cousins shun me, too, and I don't understand why. When I try to be friendly, they smirk and walk away. I wonder if they think I'm strange. Well, I do feel different from them somehow.

Cousin Francis is a few months older than I am. His name is the American version of "Francesco," that's Grampap's name, so Francis is Grampap's namesake. I figured out long ago that he is also Grampap's favorite grandchild.

Today Francis and I are sitting on the living room couch, one on each side of Grampap, and, as they talk, I'm listening. At a pause, Grampap pulls something from his pocket and presents it to Francis. I spy a quarter, and I'm eagerly anticipating mine.

But Grampap gets up and walks outside onto the porch! Slighted and humiliated, I feel a familiar sting. That's not right! Grampap is mean. Francis grins at me in triumph, and I feel a twinge of jealousy.

It's Monday, and I'm complaining to Gramma about it. "It's not fair," I whine. Patting me on the head, she says, "Aya, dona cry. Francis, he cumma only awna Sunday, anna he gets a quarter. You go toda store every daya, an every daya, I givea youa fivea cents. It'sa fair." Gramma thinks it's fair, but I don't understand her explanation. I will ask Mommy about it when I get home.

After lunch, when I'm singing songs with Aunt Millie, I interrupt her to ask, "Don't my cousins like me? They aren't nice to me." She hugs me and says, "I think they're jealous." I'm startled. "THEY are jealous of ME?" I ask, disbelieving. She smiles and says, "Yes, because you get to stay at Gramma's every day, and they don't." I've never thought of that...

Mommy explains the math to me at home, but I'm in no mood to think because I feel sick. My throat and my ears hurt, and I'm coughing. She takes my temperature and says, "You have a fever. You'll feel better after Gramma takes care of you tomorrow."

It's tomorrow. Uncle Dan delivered me and left for work. Leading me inside, Gramma says, "Aunta Toni, sheeza sicka likea you. Sheeza upstays ina bed, I tayka you upstays, too." Up we go!

"Hello, Ruth Ann, I'm sorry you're sick," says Aunt Toni, "but I'm glad you will keep me company today. I don't like missing school, but Gramma made me stay home because I'm her baby. You'll see. She knows how to make us well."

Gramma helps me into my jammies, settles me in the bed next to Aunt Toni's bed, and goes downstairs. Soon I hear her lumbering up the stairs, and, this time, she is carrying some blankets. Walking to me, she pulls my jammie tops up and places a wet flannel cloth on my chest. Then she puts another blanket on top of my covers and tucks them all under my chin.

"Oh, Gramma, it smells awful, and it burns, too."

"That'sa good, it willa mayka you sweat anna mayka da cough go way fast."

I'm already starting to sweat as Gramma moves to the next bed. Aunt Toni laughs and teases me. "Ha, ha, I get a mustard plaster, too, and we will sweat together. Isn't this fun?" I frown and shake my head no, but, if Aunt Toni thinks it's fun, I'll put up with it. I love my Aunt Toni, and I like to be with her.

When we are feeling hot to her touch, Gramma prays in Italian, makes the sign of a cross above our foreheads, and returns to the kitchen. Aunt Toni and I joke and giggle about being cooked to "well-done," and we eventually fall asleep.

Some time later, the tapping of footsteps on the stairs wakens me. It's Gramma and Aunt Millie, and they are talking in Italian. I listen, but I can't understand what they are saying. When they come into the bedroom, I chide, "Gramma, you talk so funny."

"ME? Funny? Mama mia, whaddabouda YOU? You talk wita hands," and she mimics my signing. Without hesitation, I brightly reply, "But I UNDERSTAND signing!" Gramma and Aunt Millie burst out laughing.

Hmmm. Are they making fun of me and of signing? Do all Hearing people think sign language is funny?

These thoughts begin to take root in my mind, and I am soon feeling ashamed of my parents, of their deafness, and of their signing. Now, when strangers stare at us, I feel embarrassed, even though my parents seem to take no notice. From now on, I will pretend I don't know them when we are out among Hearing people...

It's Saturday, and, before we board the streetcar to visit Deaf friends, I ask Daddy, *"May I please sit in the back?"* and he nods yes. I follow Mommy and Daddy as they take the front seats as usual. Mommy once explained their reason for choosing those seats. "Since we can't hear the motorman call the stops, we sit here to watch the street signs and recognize when it's time to get off."

After they are seated, I walk past them with eyes straight ahead, pretending I don't know them, and I take the farthest rear seat facing forward. From this position, I can watch passengers staring at Mommy and Daddy, and I can listen to their comments. I am bracing myself for ridicule, mockery, and scorn.

But, surprisingly, I don't hear any of that. Instead, I hear, "Isn't that fascinating?" and "I wish I could learn to sign," and "Nice looking couple."

Hmmm. They LIKE my parents, and they ADMIRE my parents' signing!

Before long, I get up, walk to the front, and sit beside Mother. She asks, *"Did you change your mind?"* *"Yes,"* I reply, *"and I will tell you what I hear people saying. That man across from us just said to the lady beside him, 'What a nice couple. It looks like the little girl is deaf, too.' And the pretty lady answered, 'I would love to learn sign language, it's beautiful.'"*

I keep relaying many other comments, all positive, as Mommy and Daddy smile in amusement.

When our stop is approaching, Mommy signs to me, *"For fun, here's what I want you to do. When we stand up, ready to get off, turn and face the passengers and say with a smile, 'My parents are Deaf, but I can hear. I told them everything you said, and we thank you for your kind words.'"* I follow her directions, and jaws drop as we step onto the street. I suddenly feel proud of Mother and Daddy, and of our sign language, too...

The following Saturday, Mother and I board the streetcar first and take our seats while Daddy lags behind, searching his pockets for coins to pay our fare. A man in line behind him calls loudly, "Hurry! You're holding up the line!" And, with my anxiety mounting, I watch as Daddy continues his search.

"SOME PEOPLE ARE UNCONSCIOUS," the man bellows with exasperation, and, when Daddy finally deposits his coins, everyone in line laughs. I am embarrassed for Daddy, angry at the man for his cruel remark, and upset with the others for laughing.

When Daddy sits down beside me, I tell him, *"The man in line behind you told you to hurry up, and, when you didn't move fast, he got mad and said mean things about you. Everyone laughed at you, it's not fair."* My face shows my frustration and outrage.

To my total amazement, Daddy smiles and shakes his head no. *"Don't be angry or sad when Hearing folks make fun of us or of our signing. Most of them*

are not mean; they are not aware of us. Deafness is
an invisible barrier that people cannot see."*

Daddy's kindheartedness and tolerance astound
me, and, strangely, I feel my anger begin to wilt.

Now he is looking at me in earnest, and he is signing
with great seriousness.

*"I hope, when you grow up, you will teach Hearing
people about the Deaf and Deaf culture, and
show them how to sign with us."*

I have no idea how that can ever come about...

Tonight Mother, Daddy, and I are eating supper in
our kitchen, and I'm watching their arms, hands, and
fingers flying, trying hard to understand what they
are saying. It's no use, so I complain, *"I understand
you both when you sign to me, but I don't know
what you are saying when you sign to each other.
You use new signs and sign too fast, so I am shut out
of your conversation."*

Mother speaks to me and signs at the same time so
Daddy will know what she is saying. *"Now you know
how we feel among Hearing people, especially when
we are with Gramma and Grampap and the rest of
the family. We are shut out when they are talking."*

Daddy signs, *"I understand how you feel, Ruth Ann. I
couldn't understand my mother and father when
they spoke to each other, or to me, for that matter.
It's no fun to be left out."* And, answering my
complaint, he smiles. *"Ask questions, and we will*

be happy to answer you. But, if you watch, you can often figure out the sign meanings yourself."

After supper, Mother says to me, "Now that you are a big girl, Daddy and I want to take you with us to the Club on Saturday nights. You can learn a lot of signing there. Would you like to go with us?" Puzzled, I ask, "What is 'the Club?'"and she explains. "Oh, it is the Pittsburgh Association of the Deaf, a place downtown where Deaf people meet, make friends, and have fun. 'The Club' is the short name for that place." Jumping and clapping with joy and enthusiasm, I answer, *"Yes, I want to go with you."* Mother smiles. "That's wonderful," she says with delight. "Now there's no need for you to stay with Gramma on Saturday nights..."

It's Saturday evening. Daddy locks our creaky front door behind us and drives us to downtown Pittsburgh. He parks in a dirty parking lot, and, walking under the glow of dim streetlights, we arrive at a building in sad need of repair. Mother explains, "The rent for this old building is all that we Club members can afford." Entering a dark and musty stairwell, we climb the creaky wooden stairs to the second floor.

The room is smoky, and it is filled with people "talking" with each other in sign language. I hear nothing. Wait! I do hear a laugh, and someone is coughing. And there's a stomp! Someone must be calling a friend's attention. Mother and Daddy are silently chatting with friends as I stand beside them to watch their signing.

A pretty lady waves at me. *"Hello, are you Hazels' daughter?"* I shyly shake my head yes. *"How old are you?"* I hold up four fingers. *"Can you sign?"* she asks, and I again nod yes. Soon I am looking up at a crowd of faces surrounding me, and one man is signing to the others, *"Isn't she cute? She is Hearing and just four years old. Let's test her signing."* He doesn't know that I understand his signing.

The evening's game begins. The man smiles at me and signs, *"Pay attention!"* I watch him carefully as he forms an *M* with his fingers and taps it on his chin. When I frown, puzzled, he explains, *"This is my name sign, a nickname. Most Deaf people have a name sign because using it is quicker than fingerspelling the whole name."* Pointing across the room to a fat gentleman wearing a red shirt, *M* taps a *D* on his own temple and signs, *"Please go to D and tell him that M wants to talk with him."* I see Daddy is watching me, so I look at him questioningly. He smiles and signs his permission. *"It's O-K, you can do what M says."*

I start on my way and pass many smiling eyes. When I reach *D*, I tug at his shirt, interrupting him as he is signing with a friend. He looks down at me with raised eyebrows and a startled smile as I sign *M*'s message, and, with a grin, he signs back, *"You tell M that D is busy now, but I will see him in five minutes."* I return to *M* with *D*'s reply. Back and forth I go to a number of people, using a variety of name signs and carrying many messages. I'm having fun! The game ends when Daddy signs to me, *"Time to go home,"* so I smile, throw a kiss, and wave goodbye to my new friends.

When we arrive home, I ask Mother, "What is your name sign?" She forms an *S* with her fingers and places it on the left side of her chest. "This stands for 'Schifino,'" she says. "When I was in high school, my friends gave that sign to me."

Expectantly, I ask, *"What is MY name sign?"*

"Oh," she says, "Daddy and I did not give you name sign because we want people to know your real name." That makes sense to me.

With each visit to the Club, my sign vocabulary increases, and I am more at ease. Some of the Club members are like Mother, they sign while speaking English sentences. Others, like Daddy, sign with no voice, and their signing doesn't follow English at all. So, in my mind, I have to change their signing into English to know what they are saying. No two people sign exactly alike, and I'm learning to use and understand varieties of signing. When I make a mistake, my Club friends correct me in a teasing way, and, when I do well, they clap and cheer. I love my Deaf family, for everyone is kind and patient.

I do not yet realize that I am in the midst of a unique and fascinating culture...

This Saturday's chores are done, and Daddy says, *"We are going on the streetcar to visit Mr. and Mrs. Mayer. We have no way of finding out if they are home, so we will take a chance and travel there. If they are not home, we will try to visit the Scotts."*

We arrive at Mr. and Mrs. Mayer's house, and Daddy rings the doorbell. Peering through the front window, we see their doorbell lights flashing, but no one answers the door. I watch in fascination as Mother opens the door of a small box hanging beside their front door. Removing a notepad and a pencil, she writes something, puts the pad and pencil back in the box, and closes its little door.

On the way to visit Mr. and Mrs. Scott, Mother explains, "My note said, 'Sorry we missed you. We will try again next Saturday.' Most of our Deaf friends have little boxes hanging outside their front doors. I dream of a day when we won't need these boxes, for Deaf people will somehow be able to contact friends in advance to make sure they will be home."

When we arrive at their house, Mrs. Scott answers the door. *"What a nice surprise, please come in,"* she signs. *"K is playing golf, and he will be sorry he missed you."* As we settle on the couch, two Hearing youths come into the living room, and Mrs. Scott introduces them. *"This is our son, Ned, he is seventeen, and this is our daughter, Jean, she is twelve."* With a croaky voice, Mrs. Scott introduces us to them. "This is Mr. and Mrs. Hazel and their daughter, Ruth Ann." Ned and Jean smile politely, nod at us, and then speak loudly to their mother.

Twisting his mouth in greatly exaggerated lip movements, Ned says, "I'm going to the movies, and I'll be back later." I watch the ugly spectacle in amazement. Then, Jean, in like manner, says, "I am going to my friend Rachel's house, I'll be home for supper." Mrs. Scott frowns as she stares intently at their lips in an effort to lipread. Ned and Jean quickly disappear, leaving me astonished! Mrs. Scott's kids don't sign! I wonder why.

Mrs.Scott must notice the shock on my face, for she explains. *"Ned refuses to sign at all, and he gives us a lot of worry. He sneaks out his window at night while K and I are asleep, and he gets into trouble with the police. And Jean demands, 'Don't ever sign with me in front of anyone.'"* Mother signs,*"Sorry"* and tactfully changes the subject. As they continue their conversation, I am watching them to study their signing.

Mrs. Scott turns to me. *"Your mother tells me you go with your parents to the Club every week. How do you like it?"* I reply, *"Yes, I go to the Club. The members are teaching me many signs, and I like it very much."* Mrs. Scott says, "Good for you." I see regret in her face.

After a while, Mother and Daddy rise to leave, and I follow them, waiting as they linger at the door with Mrs. Scott to finish their conversation. Then, we say goodbye and hurry to catch the streetcar.

On our way home, I question Mother, *"Why don't the Scott children sign?"*

She looks sad as she explains, "They are ashamed of their parents and of signing. I'm glad you don't feel that way."

I nod with understanding and decide not to press the subject further. A twinge of guilt reminds me of the shame I once felt. I'm so glad I never told anyone about it because I don't feel that way anymore. Still, I know full well how those kids feel.

Active social clubs, a visual language, common customs, and the need for communicating effectively with the Hearing World—so far, this is my brief introduction to Deaf culture. Mother says there is much more to learn...

It's another Saturday, Daddy is home, and he allows me to nap on the big bed. I have an earache again, and, as usual, he announces brightly, "Here comes Dr. Quack!" and he gives me a dose of medicine. I beg, *"Please, Daddy, tell me a story so it won't hurt so much."* He sits down beside me and explains. *"I don't know fairy tales, but I can tell you a real story about the time I was a little boy. Is that O-K with you?"* I eagerly nod yes, so Daddy smacks his lips to get ready to speak, and he begins to tell his story.

"My family rarely talked to me, and, when they did, they used gestures. I never knew what to expect. One day, when I was five years old, my mother packed a suitcase and dressed me in a nice suit."

"My father carried the suitcase and took me for a ride on a train. As I watched all the fields and towns passing by, I discovered I could hear the wheels clacking on the tracks and the train whistle blowing. I was SO excited! I tried to tell my father, but he didn't understand me."

"Soon the train stopped, we got off, and my father led me into a big building, the Ohio School for the Deaf. A man met us and spoke to my father while a nice lady gave me candy. After I finished eating the candy, I turned to my father, but he was walking out the door!"

"I started to run after him, but the man held me back. After I ate supper, he took me to a bedroom shared by a group of boys and gestured that I was to sleep in one of the empty beds. I thought, 'My father and mother don't want me,' and I cried myself to sleep. But I learned to sign with my classmates, and my teachers signed, too. After that, I didn't want to go home where no one signed. I was the happiest at school."

"*More, more,*" I beg, so he continues. "I was chosen to be the drummer boy, so I led my classmates in our march to the chapel every morning where we heard Bible stories and learned about right and wrong, then went to our classes. I enjoyed my studies, and I was a good student. There were afterschool activities, too. I played tennis, and I was a star on the wrestling team, but, best of all, I enjoyed being a member of the debate team. So, you see, after being lonely at home, I had many friends at school. "

"All the boys were taught a trade, like carpentry or printing, and I chose printing because my father was a printer. I can work on the Linotype and Monotype machines. Without signing, I would not be able to do all those things. Now you can understand how sign language saved my life!"

"Many years ago, Hearing people thought that Deaf children could not learn, but they were wrong. With signing, deaf children can learn easily."

"We Deaf people are not stupid, we just have a different language."

My eyes are closing, heavy with sleep, as I hear Dr. Quack walk out of the room and close the door. The sound of his footsteps descending the stairs fades in the distance as sleep overtakes me...

It's Sunday night, my ears still ache, and I'm having trouble swallowing. Dr. Quack tucks me in bed and gives me another dose of medicine. *"Please tell me another story,"* I plead, *"It helps me forget my hurt,"* and Daddy obliges. Sitting beside me, he smacks his lips as he often does when he is preparing to speak.

"I was born a twin, and my twin brother died at birth, but I had an older brother, Paul, and an older sister, Edna. Paul did not talk with me often, but my sister learned to fingerspell, so she helped me talk to my parents when she could. I didn't see much of my family because, when I was in my early twenties, I met a nice Deaf girl, the daughter of Hearing parents. She was a Linotype operator at the same Omaha, Nebraska printing plant where I worked, and that is where we met."

"After we were married, I built a beautiful house for us. We were happily married for ten years when she became ill with a blood disease, and she died. We had no children, so I was left alone in the house. It was a sad and lonely time for me. Then, luckily, I met Irene five years later at a convention of the Deaf here in downtown Pittsburgh, and I courted her by driving my Model A Ford back and forth on dirt roads between Omaha and Pittsburgh. It's a good thing the NAD was fighting for the right of Deaf people to drive a car."

"When we married, I took Irene to live in my home in Omaha, but, soon afterward, the printing plant closed, I lost my job, I couldn't pay the bills, and the bank took our house. That's when I got ulcers, so your mother and I decided to move to Pittsburgh to be near her family."

"Where is YOUR family?" I ask, and Daddy replies, "My parents died long before you were born. I lost track of Paul, and Edna lives near Chicago, so I've never lived close to either of them."

Hmmm. I can't imagine myself without Gramma and the rest of Mother's family close by.

My face is sad at Daddy's story until he says, "Yes, there has been sadness in my life, but I stopped thinking about it a long time ago. It is a waste of time. I am happier now than ever before because I have YOU! You are the light of my life, and I worship you." He kisses my forehead.

Daddy's words touch my heart. If he worships me, I must live up to his expectations.

"Now it is time for you to rest and get well. Sweet dreams," he says, and, after giving me a hug, Dr. Quack makes his exit, and I close my heavy eyes in thought and wonder until sleep takes over.

My earaches waken me. Surrounded by darkness, I call, "Daddy! Daddy!" even though I know he can't hear me. I need his comfort, so I try to climb out of my crib to tap him, but I'm weak, it hurts to move my head, and my ears are throbbing. I'm alone with my pain. I pull the covers over my head and curl up, moaning, "Daddy, Daddy, Daddy," until sleep quiets me...

This afternoon we are at Pittsburgh Children's Hospital where doctors are probing my throat and ears with cold steel instruments. It hurts! They talk quietly among themselves and then one doctor speaks to Mother who is lipreading.

"Your daughter's tonsils are infected. If we don't remove them, the infection will spread to her ears and may damage her hearing. We recommend that we take her tonsils out immediately, and, if you agree, we will schedule her surgery for Monday morning at seven." Mother relays the doctors' recommendation to Daddy, and, without hesitation, they sign papers. I wonder what "tonsils" are.

When we get home, Mother takes me aside and explains about tonsils and what will happen to me on Monday. "You are going to have 'surgery.' After your tonsils are gone, you will have no more sore throats and no earaches. Won't that be wonderful?" I nod yes, but I think my face shows my uneasiness because Daddy hugs me and cheerfully says, "Push that worry away." Then, with both hands, he dramatically sweeps the worry aside as I giggle. It seems as if Mother and Daddy think that this surgery is nothing to be concerned about, so I'm not worried. I'll be SO happy to stop hurting.

In the dark of early morning, we arrive at the hospital. Footsteps echo in the empty lobby as a man wearing a white coat appears and smiles at us. He shakes Daddy's hand and then speaks to Mother while she reads his lips. I am listening from Daddy's arms.

"Good morning, I'm Dr. Soros, the surgeon who will remove your daughter's tonsils. You and your husband may stay at her bedside until we take her to surgery, but, after that, you must sit in the waiting room. We will call you when the operation is over."

Mother tells Daddy what the doctor said and then tells me, "You will go to sleep, and, when you wake up, we will be there with some ice cream."

A nurse appears and leads me away as I wave and throw a kiss to Mother and Daddy. I'm on my own, and it's a familiar feeling.

I lie on a table looking up into bright lights. I can't see anything, but I hear people talking. A nurse wearing a mask bends over me and puts a cup over my nose.

"Hello, big girl, you and I will have a good time together with this game. Are you ready?" I nod yes, and she gives me directions.

"When I say 'ONE,' take a big breath; when I say 'TWO,' take a big breath; and when I say 'THREE,' take another big breath. You will smell something funny called Ether, and it will help you fall asleep."

"When you wake up, your throat will hurt, but ice cream will make it feel better."

"May I please have chocolate?" I ask, and she laughs. "You sure can, honey, here we go!" She starts to count. At "ONE," a buzzing starts in my head; at "TWO," I feel like I'm spinning in space. I don't hear "THREE."

I waken in a fog, my head is buzzing, and Mother

Ruth Ann at Four

and Daddy are standing beside my bed. *"My throat hurts when I swallow,"* I sign. "Ice cream will help," says Mother, and Daddy chants, "Here comes the 'Kissing Bug'" as he gives me a cup of chocolate ice cream and plants a kiss on my forehead.

I'm home from the hospital when Daddy confides, *"I've been praying that you will not become deaf."*

"That would be O-K," I assure him. *"Then I would be like you and Mother and our Deaf friends at the Club."*

Chapter 2

GROWTH

At supper Dad says, *"Thank you, Ruth Ann, for telling the family what I sign and for signing what they say.* Mother adds, "And I'm happy, too, when you sign for me, especially if I can't read their lips." She continues.

"When you speak, or 'voice,' for a signer and sign for a speaker, AND you don't leave anything out or put your own words in, you are 'interpreting.' Deaf people need interpreters. That's why I teach sign language at the library every week. I hope my students will become good sign language interpreters. Would you like to be a good interpreter for Dad and me?" I eagerly nod yes. "OK, then please remember this," she cautions.

"When you voice for Dad's signing, don't just watch his hands and fingers, watch his facial expressions, his eyes, his body motions, and his gestures. They will help you understand what he means and how he feels. Is he sad, or happy, or excited, or angry? Use your voice to show that feeling. And, when you are signing for someone who is talking to me, listen carefully to that speaker's voice. Does it sound sad, happy, excited, or angry? Make your signing, body movements, eye glances, and facial expressions clearly show it."

"*O-K,*" I say, "*I will remember to do what you have told me. I do want to be a good interpreter for you and Dad.*"...

It's a bright Sunday morning in fall, and Dad says to me, "*You are almost five years old. That's old enough to attend Sunday school, so I am taking you to the church down the hill this morning.*" Mother helps me get dressed in my good clothes and explains, "It's the Blackadore Avenue Presbyterian Church."

I'm so excited! I've seen that building, but I've never been inside. I'm curious because I know all Mother's relatives go to a church, but it's not this one. After breakfast, Dad takes my hand, and we walk down Perchment Street, turn left at Blackadore Avenue, and arrive at the white building on the corner.

A man wearing a suit is standing outside the wide open church doors, and he is politely greeting people. At our turn, Dad offers his trusty notepad. After the man reads the message on it, he nods and disappears inside.

Now a different man comes to greet us, and I interpret. "Good morning, I am Mr. Craft, the Sunday school superintendent. You want to enroll your daughter, is that right?" My face shows his questioning to Dad.

Dad nods yes, and I voice as he signs. "*My name is Edwin Hazel. My wife and I are Deaf, and we don't attend here because we can't hear the sermon. But we would like to enroll our Hearing daughter, Ruth Ann, in your Sunday school. She will come here alone.*"I sign as Mr. Craft replies, "We will be happy to have Ruth Ann in our Sunday school." He gives Dad a paper to fill out. Dad writes on it and returns it. After reading the document carefully, Mr. Craft asks, "May I have your phone number?" I sign his request.

I'm surprised at what Dad does next. He shakes his head no, raises his eyebrows, gestures with both palms up, and shrugs his shoulders. Mr. Craft understands him! The superintendent's face gets red, and, as I sign his reply, I make my face and eyes show his embarrassment. "Oh! I'm sorry. I see; you don't have a telephone."

Now he speaks to me, and I interpret for Dad. "Ruth Ann, we look forward to seeing you next Sunday at nine o'clock, and I will be waiting for you at this door." I thank him, Dad smiles, they shake hands, and we start back home...

It's the following Saturday, and Mother and I are in the living room doing our weekly chores. She is using the Electrolux vacuum sweeper, and I'm dusting when I hear a knock at the front door. I wave at Mother, point to the door, and she opens it to see a pretty lady smiling at her. I signal Mother to turn the sweeper off; she has no idea it is so noisy.

When the lady starts to speak, I see Mother reading her lips, so I keep still. "I'm Mrs. Baker," the lady says. "I will be Ruth Ann's Sunday school teacher, and I have come to welcome her to my class." Mother smiles and says, "Please come in," and she gestures for the lady to sit on our couch. Then Mother takes a seat in the easy chair and beckons me to stand beside her. Now we both are facing Mrs. Baker.

My teacher's eyes scan our meager furnishings and then focus on me. "I'm glad to meet you, Ruth Ann. I brought you a magazine with pictures, and you can keep it." Mother responds, "Thank you, that is very thoughtful of you, and we appreciate your kindness." I say thank you, too. After exchanging niceties, Mrs. Baker rises to say, "I must go to another appointment now, but I look forward to seeing you tomorrow, Ruth Ann." Mother escorts her to the door, and, after Mrs. Baker leaves, I finish my chores and sit in the easy chair to pore over the magazine she brought me. I'm excited and in a hurry for Sunday to dawn...

It's morning, and I awaken early with eager anticipation. Mother dresses me in a pretty suit and new shoes, and Dad walks me to the church. Mr. Craft is waiting at the door, just as he promised. Returning Dad's salute, he addresses me, and I interpret for Dad.

"Good morning, Ruth Ann, I've been waiting for you. Come, I will take you to your class." Dad smiles and nods, I kiss him goodbye, and I follow Mr. Craft down a hallway. I'm on another adventure—alone.

"This is your Sunday school room," he says as he opens a door and ushers me inside a bright and sunny room. Mrs. Baker is playing the piano, and boys and girls are sitting on the floor behind her, singing. She smiles at us, and, when the song ends, she turns to introduce me. "Boys and girls, this is Ruth Ann Hazel, our new class member, let's welcome her," and they all clap. As Mr. Craft slips out the door, my teacher motions for me to sit on the floor with the others.

She shows us a picture in her book. "Today's story is about Jesus," she says, and she points to the kind-looking man with a beard and a little girl sitting on his lap. "This is Jesus, and He is saying, 'Let the little children come to me.' He loves each of us, and, although we can't see Him, He is our Friend, and He is with us always." My ears perk up! I need such a friend! And now that I know Jesus loves me and is always with me, I won't ever have to feel alone.

Dad is waiting when Sunday school is over, and he asks, *"How did you like Sunday School?"* I reply, *"I liked it a lot. My teacher told us a Bible story about Jesus."* Dad smiles and says, *"Good."* I don't tell him that Jesus is my new Friend. That will be my secret...

Blackadore Avenue Church

We just celebrated my fifth birthday, and I am enrolled in kindergarten at Crescent Elementary School. This weekend we are moving down the hill to Frankstown Avenue. When I asked why we are moving, Dad said it's because our new apartment is closer to my school, and that means a shorter walk for me. What's more, I will have my own bedroom. I'm thrilled!

We have a five-room apartment on the second floor of a house owned by a Deaf couple, and they live on the first floor. There is one front door, a wide foyer, and an open stairway to the right of the entry leads up to our apartment. At the top of the stairs, there is an exposed hallway that leads to our rooms. At the front end of that hall is my bedroom, and it has a window overlooking Frankstown Avenue. I have a regular bed, a chest of drawers with a mirror, and a little chair.

When I stand in the hallway outside my bedroom and peer over the railing, I can see the stairs leading down to the first floor landing, and I can see the front door.

An unexpected thought enters my mind as I take in that view: I must always listen, especially at night, to keep all the Deaf people in this house safe.

While Mother and Dad are busy getting settled, I wander outside and discover a narrow alleyway that runs between our house and the house next door. Curious, I decide to see where it leads. I pass our house and our fenced yard and come to another alley running left and right along a chicken wire fence bordering the backyards of row houses. Turning left,

I pass five houses and make a surprising discovery: Gramma's backyard! I can't believe it!

No one answers the back door, so I turn and race back home. Dashing up the stairs, I excitedly tell Mother, "I can walk through the alley to Gramma's house, it's very close."

"Yes, it is," she says, "now please listen carefully. On school days, walk to Gramma's, leave your lunch bag with her, and walk to school. Go back to her house for lunch and then return to school afterward. But, when school is over in the afternoon, do not go to Gramma's again. Come straight here and change into your playclothes. After that, you can choose to go to Gramma's, or you can decide to stay right here, whichever you would like to do."

"But, if you go to Gramma's, you must be here when I get home from work at six o'clock. I will tell that to her. And you must always be sure to lock the door behind you."

On my first day of kindergarten, Daddy reviews the plan, pins the house key to my undershirt, hugs me, and sends me on my way. After school is out in the afternoon, I bypass Conemaugh street and walk down Frankstown Avenue to our new apartment. I have already memorized our brand new address: 8118 Frankstown Avenue. I feel SO grown up with my new independence. I use my key to enter the house, and I lock the door behind me.

Changing into my afterschool playclothes, I make my choice: I don't want to go to Gramma's to play today, I think I'll stay home.

I curl up in a comfortable living room chair. Beside it, on a little half-moon table, is my brand new Zenith radio. As darkness descends, I contentedly listen to one program after another: "The Lone Ranger," "Superman," "Orphan Annie," "One Man's Family," and "Jack Armstrong." But, when Mother arrives home, I turn the radio off and help her set the table...

This apartment fascinates me. It has a modern kitchen, a complete bathroom, and lots of electric outlets. I'm curious about electricity after watching Dad work with his gadgets. He cautioned me to respect electric outlets and warned me not to fool with them. Nevertheless, I've been wondering what will happen if I stick one of Mother's bobby pins into the slots of an outlet.

So tonight, after Mother and Dad tuck me in and retire, I slip out of bed, and, by the light from the downstairs foyer, I cautiously creep into our hallway. I pull the chair from my bedroom and place it under the wall light fixture. An outlet is in its base, and it is near the closed door of Mother and Dad's bedroom.

I climb up on the chair, bobby pin in hand, and spread the prongs, placing one in the left slot and the other in the right slot. Instantly, a shockwave of electricity flashes through my body with a loud BUZZ, and my hand automatically yanks the bobby pin out of the slots as I recoil in terror. Did Dad hear the noise? No, he's snoring. Oh, I am SO relieved! No one will ever know what I did.

Climbing down carefully, I return my chair to its rightful place and meekly crawl into bed. This venture into mischief has not turned out so well. My conscience convicts me, and, drifting to sleep, I resolve never to disobey again. I don't ever want to disappoint Mother and Dad...

It's nearing Christmas, and I hear an announcement on my radio. With every new subscription, the Pittsburgh Press is offering a free baby doll. The description of that doll captures my heart, and I tell Mother and Dad about it, begging, *"Please start a subscription to the newspaper so I can have that little doll."*

But Mother replies, "We don't have the money to pay for the newspaper, Ruth Ann." And Dad has the same answer: *"The newspaper is too expensive."* He picks me up, hugs me tight, and tickles me. My squeals of laughter erase the subject from my mind—temporarily.

Soon I am feeling sorry for myself. Mother and Dad always say no. "No, you can't have a puppy." "No, you can't have a kitty." "No, you can't have that dolly." Well, Santa knows my wish, so maybe he will bring that dolly to me. I was naughty only once this year.

It's Christmas Eve, our decorated tree is in the living room, and I'm ready for bed. What was that? There's a loud rapping on my bedroom window! I must run and alert Mother and Dad. I find Mother in the kitchen and warn her about the noise. She calmly says, "That's probably Santa Claus telling you to go to bed. He never goes inside a home until the children are asleep."

I'm amazed! Santa? Outside my window? I scurry to bed, certain that Santa is watching my every move. Snuggling under my blankets, I close my eyes as visions of that beautiful dolly twirl in my head, and I am soon fast asleep.

Little do I know that it is Dad outside tapping on my window. He is standing on the roof that hangs over our front porch.

It's early Christmas morning, and I hurry to the living room. Oh! The doll I longed for is sitting under our tree, smiling at me. With eyes only for her, I run and swoop her into my arms, soon becoming aware that a child-size desk and chair, a toy piano, and a shaggy toy doggie are sitting beside our tree. I am SO happy! Santa Claus didn't disappoint me. I run to Mother and Dad, jumping and clapping for joy. *"Look what Santa brought me,"* I giggle. They are nodding and smiling at my excitement.

And, lo and behold, we begin to receive the daily newspaper. Mother reads it from cover to cover. I read, too. My books are stories Aunt Millie has read to me, like "Aesop's Fables," "Cinderella," and "Pinocchio." Mother reads poems to me, too. My favorite poem is "The Night Before Christmas..."

It's June 1939, and my kindergarten year is ending. Mother is home from work this afternoon, and I am walking back to school with her. She says, "We are going to see your kindergarten teacher, Miss Wooley. She wants to talk with me. Please be ready to sign if I need you." I nod yes and sign, *"I will."*

Ruth Ann at Five

We climb the cement steps, enter the big double doors, and pass empty classrooms until we reach Miss Wooley's room. She is waiting for us, and she smiles and shakes Mother's hand. When she starts to speak, Mother's glance signals she is unable to read Miss Wooley's lips, so I sign as my teacher talks to Mother about ME! Her voice is soft and kind, and she sounds sorry, so my face shows it, just as Mother has taught me.

"Mrs. Hazel, the school made a mistake last year by accepting Ruth Ann in kindergarten. The state law specifies that a child must be five on or before September 1 to be accepted, and she was still four on that date. In other words, she did not turn five until after the deadline, so she did not qualify to enroll. This means that Ruth Ann must stay in my class another year."

After a studied pause, Mother replies with a calm and pleasant voice, "Oh, I see. Well, we will follow the state law." And, addressing me, she says brightly, "Ruth Ann, you are lucky! You will be in kindergarten with Miss Wooley again next year." I clap with joy at this exciting news.

Miss Wooley speaks cheerily to me, and I am smiling as I interpret for Mother. "Ruth Ann, you will be my special helper with the new students, and you and I will have lots of fun." The thought of being my teacher's helper thrills me!

On the walk back home, Mother grins and says, "I will let you tell everyone the good news, and it will be your happy surprise." I nod gleefully and announce, "I know what I want to be when I grow up. I want to be a teacher, just like Miss Wooley." Mother says, "That will be wonderful," and I spring ahead of her to skip all the way home...

I like to play with the kids on Conemaugh Street. I'm younger, but they include me because I'm at Gramma's house so much of the time. We are a mixed bunch: half are colored, and the rest of us are second generation Italians—except me. I'm half

Italian from Mother's side, and half English from Dad's side. We kids have lots of fun playing group games, like kick-the-can, sardines, and red rover. On holiday nights, we play hide-and-seek in the dark alleys behind the row houses until we hear a loud voice calling someone to come home.

Marie's folks are Italian, and they live a few doors from Gramma. Even though Marie is two years older than I am, we are good friends. We roller skate and jump rope, and we play jacks and hopscotch for hours, too. Sometimes she tries to cheat, but Aunt Toni told me I must not let Marie do that. I am to speak back and not allow her to boss me. I tried it, and it works!

I know who lives in every house on this block. In the last house in the row live Mr. and Mrs. Washington, a nice old colored couple. I think they are old because Mr. Washington has a white beard and white hair, and his wife has white hair, too. They're usually sitting in their rocking chairs on their porch. I wave to them every day—once on my way to the store for Gramma, and again on my way back with grocery items.

Gramma explained why she needs to send me to the store every day. She doesn't know how to read or write, so she can't make shopping lists like Mother does. I don't want to be in that predicament, so I'm working hard to learn how to read and write. I don't complain about going to the store every day because Gramma gives me a nickel after each trip.

Today I am on my way to the store, and, when I get to Mr. and Mrs. Washington's house, I see Mrs.

Washington sitting on the porch alone. I wave and call, "Where is Mr. Washington?" She is motioning that I come up on the porch, so I mount the two steps and go to her. "Mr. Washington is dead," she says softly. I am shocked, and I don't know what to do. "Would you like to say goodbye to him?" she asks. I'm not sure what she means, but I want to please her, so I nod yes.

She takes my hand and leads me through the rickety front screen door, and it slams behind us as we walk into her parlor. Heavy drapes hide the windows, covering the room in darkness, and, when my eyes can see, I am startled. There is Mr. Washington, lying in a box! He is wearing a suit, and a white blanket covers the lower part of his body. I've never seen a dead person, but I'm not afraid. I'm sad.

No one else is in the room, so I ask, "Where are your children? Where is your family?" She shakes her head and says sadly, "I don't have any." I feel sorry for Mrs. Washington, so I clasp her bony wrinkled hand, and, looking at the body of her dead husband, I say, "Goodbye, Mr. Washington. I will miss you." With tears brimming, Mrs. Washington hugs me and leads me back outside. At the bottom of the steps, I turn, throw a kiss to her, and continue on my way. A new and strange feeling sweeps over me.

Back from the store, I give Gramma the groceries and tell her the story. "Tsk, tsk, poor Mrs. Washinaton," she says sorrowfully. "I willa senda summa chicken anna ravioli to her." And Aunt Millie says, "I will add a nice card to let Mrs. Washington know we feel sympathy for her." Sympathy! Maybe that's the word for my overwhelming feeling.

On Conemaugh Street, I am with adults and kids who love and care about each other, and it feels good.

Gramma and Ruth Ann 1939

Chapter 3

LESSONS

I'm a big girl now—six and a half—and I'm watching Dad with anticipation. He is sitting in the living room easy chair browsing the "Reader's Digest." I suspect he will ask me about a word he comes across and then we will play our dictionary game.

I was right! Dad looks at me and says, *"Here is a new word,"* and he fingerspells *"s-t-a-t-u-t-e."* *"Do you know what the word means?"* I shake my head no. "Let's GO!" he cries out as he leads the way to our family dictionary. *"You look it up. It begins with an 's,' so where will you find it?"*

Dad showed me long ago how words are arranged here by their first letter in A-B-C order, so I turn to the back of the book and find "s" words. Dad finds the word, "statute." "Look," he says, "here is the meaning: it is a law or rule." He has trouble pronouncing "statute," and I'm trying to say it using the sounds of the letters Miss Wooley taught me.

"Can you fingerspell this word and then use it in a sentence?" he asks. *"I think I can,"* I say. I look at the word while I fingerspell it. *"'S-t-a-t-u-t-e' means 'l-a-w.'"* Dad claps for me.

"It is good to learn new words. In high school, I always carried a dictionary in my pocket."

"*My friends and classmates enjoyed teasing me about it, and they called me a 'walking dictionary,' but I didn't mind. The dictionary is a good friend.*"

"*Why do you want to learn new words?*"

"*Because my signed language does not use words to be heard, it uses movements to be seen. The sign for 'l-a-w' or 's-t-a-t-u-t-e' is this,*" and he forms an *L* with his right hand and taps it on his left palm. "*Learning new English words helps me to read and write better, and it will do the same for you.*"

Dad points his index finger up, so I wait. He runs downstairs to the basement and returns carrying a small box by its handle. Putting the box on his desk, he removes its top to reveal a record player, and, from a pocket in the lid, he draws a 78 RPM record.

Placing it on the spindle, he starts the recording and says, "*Tell me what you hear.*" I listen and report, "*A man is talking about a c-h-a-r-t, and he says people should buy it.*" Excitedly, Dad says, "That's right!"

Opening his desk drawer, he removes a big white card folded into three long sections, and he unfolds the card to reveal many words. There is a dial in the center of the open card, and Dad spins it, announcing, "This is 'Hazel's Parliamentary Law Chart.' See all these words? They answer fifteen hundred parliamentary law questions. I invented this chart before you were born, and I sold it to Deaf leaders. I wanted to sell it to Hearing people, too, but I knew no one would understand my speaking, so I paid this man to record my sales talk. I carried my suitcase from business to business, playing the record and selling hundreds of charts. So, you see? Words have power."

"What is 'p-a-r...l-a-w?" (I fumble the fingerspelling.)

"Parliamentary laws are the statutes people should follow during their meetings in order to get things done in a fair way and without confusion. I have studied and taught parliamentary law for many years."

"Why?"

"It is because we who are Deaf must work together effectively to overcome the prejudice and discrimination of Hearing people. When we follow parliamentary statutes, we make faster progress."

Dad knows a lot about statutes, and I am fascinated by words...

Edwin and His Parliamentary Law Chart

Mother has come to me this evening with a request from a friend.

"Mrs. Whitehall has a doctor's appointment on Saturday morning at ten o'clock, and she wants you to interpret for her. She and Mr. Whitehall will pick you up and drive you to Dr. Victor's office, and, when her visit is over, they will bring you home."

"I don't think I can do it," I protest, "I've never interpreted for anyone except you and Dad."

"You're seven years old, and I think you can handle this. Besides, Mrs. Whitehall says you two understand each other well when you chat at the Club. She begs you to please go with her."

Begs? Mrs. Whitehall's plea touches my heart, and I agree to do the job. I tell Mother I will try my best.

All day Friday I'm uneasy, "What ifs?" fill my mind. What if I don't understand the doctor? What if I don't understand Mrs. Whitehall's signs? Then, I remember Dad's advice and push the worry aside.

It's Saturday, and I spring out of bed. Dad is cheerful, and, after I'm dressed and finish breakfast, he hugs me and says, "You are kind, and I am proud of you. Just do your best." I do my best, all goes smoothly, and Mrs. Whitehall and Dr. Victor are pleased. Best of all, I realize it was easier than I expected, and my concerns were a waste of time.

Before long, my Saturdays are filled with interpreting jobs. I go with our Club friends to doctors, to dentists, to lawyers, to landlords, and even to Hearing relatives.

I interpret for my parents and the Hearing people they talk with wherever we go, too. To my surprise, I enjoy these grownup situations because I'm learning new words and new signs. My world is expanding...

I am eight when we arrive at the Club to find the president waiting for us at the top of the stairs. He says to me, *"Tonight, there will be a presentation by a Hearing man, and we would like to have you interpret his speech for us."*

I look at him in horror and shake my head no, but he persists. *"Please, we all know you will do a good job. Besides, there is no one else here who can do it."* I'm cornered, and I'm frightened by the idea, but, with Mother and Dad's encouragement, I reluctantly agree to interpret.

Gathering my courage, I stand on the platform beside the speaker, a man dressed in a suit and a necktie. He smiles and introduces himself as the owner of the building, and he thanks me for interpreting for him. I nervously smile in return, face all my Deaf friends sitting in rows, and try to forget all those eyes looking at me. I manage to sign his twenty-minute talk as he explains why he must raise the rent.

His speech finally ends, and Club members come to me, saying, *"Thank you for the good job."*

Hmmm. Was my interpreting really good? Well, they nodded with understanding and reacted in the right places. Those are comforting thoughts.

It's a few months later, and we arrive at the Club to see a stage set up, and several Deaf people are in costume. A crowd of people sit in rows of chairs facing the stage, and I hear voices of Hearing people. I tell Mother, and she goes to find out what is happening. She returns to say, "I've just been told there will be a play presented by a Deaf cast, and Hearing family members are in the audience. The actors and actresses want you to voice their signing for their Hearing relatives."

A play? Questions flood my mind. What is the story? Where does it take place? Who are the characters? There's no time to ask and no time to be nervous. One of the members hurries me to a seat in the front row where I can see the signs, fingerspelling, gestures, and facial expressions clearly. As we walk, I'm quickly reviewing what Mother taught me: to match my voice to the signer; to watch face, eyes, and gestures; to show expressed feelings by using the tone of my voice.

The play starts, so I take a deep breath and proceed. The signing is fast-paced, so my body is on high alert, and my eyes are sharply focused, for a blink might cause me to miss a sign or fingerspelling. I'm changing my voice quickly and often: I'm the king's deep voice, the queen's soft voice, the child's high voice. Now I sound angry, now joyful, now distressed, now teasing. I can't believe I am doing this! I'm wound up tight inside, I feel sick, and my head hurts. At the break, I hurry to the restroom and try to calm down by splashing cold water on my face, but it doesn't help. I return to my seat, still feeling queasy and tense as the next scene starts.

When the play finally ends, I sigh with relief and sink back in my chair, quivering inside. Several Hearing folks approach me and say, "Thank you, dear, for your interpreting, you did a beautiful job." I'm so upset that I'm tempted to answer, "How do YOU know? You can't read signing to see if I spoke correctly," but, instead, I politely say, "Thank you."

The Club president comes to thank me, too, and, when Mother and Dad gaze at me proudly, I hide my true feelings. I don't want to spoil their joy.

The next day we are at Gramma's, and, while everyone is chatting noisily, I pull Aunt Toni aside and describe last night's experience. "There was no one else to interpret, so I didn't have the heart to say no. It was SO difficult, and, after the play was over, I felt weak."

Aunt Toni turns abruptly, and, before I can stop her, she walks to Dad and taps his shoulder. Oh, NO! I don't want her to talk to Dad about it. I anxiously wait until she returns with her report.

"I spoke, fingerspelled, and gestured. Pointing to you, I said, 'Don't *f-o-r-c-e* her to *i-n-t-e-r-p-r-e-t,* she's just a *l-i-t-t-l-e* girl, it's too *h-a-r-d* for her.' But your dad just smiled and said, 'Don't worry, Ruth Ann interprets very well, it's easy for her.' Then, he walked away. I couldn't convince him."

I'm relieved that Dad doesn't think I complained to Aunt Toni, I don't want to disappoint him. "Thanks for trying to help," I tell her, "but I didn't want you to speak to Dad. I wasn't complaining, I just
79

wanted sympathy." I laugh nervously and joke, "I'm a talking dolly, just push the 'start' button, and I will interpret."

As we laugh, a wave of guilt engulfs me. Maybe I WAS complaining. The guilt lingers with me for days...

Ruth Ann at Nine

It's spring, and we are attending a Club-sponsored picnic at Kennywood Amusement Park. While Mother and the ladies prepare lunch for the group, Dad takes my hand and says, "Let's go for a ride on the roller coaster, it's called, *'T-h-e R-a-c-e-r.'*" As we hurry toward the ticket booth, I gaze up at the tracks that rise high in the air, and I feel a bit uneasy.

Noisy crowds are milling as we stand in a long line to buy tickets. Finally, with tickets in hand, Dad leads me to the first seat in the front car. After a man collects our tickets, Dad pulls the car's restraining bar to our laps, and the car lurches forward.

As we start to ascend, riders start screaming, and the uproar terrifies me, so I tap Dad's shoulder and sign, *"I'm afraid, I want to get off."* But he laughs and says, "Too late, we must stay. Don't worry." I take a deep breath and grab the bar tightly as our car continues its climb.

Click, click, click! Up we go as the cars slowly rise on the steep tracks. The shouting resonates in my ears, and all I can see is the sky. There is no turning back! When the car reaches the top and begins its steep descent, I hang on for dear life.

Hmmm. Sometimes interpreting feels like that...

On Friday, my third grade class is dismissed at three o'clock, and the Crescent School crossing guard helps me cross Route 380. I bypass Conemaugh Street, and I'm walking on Frankstown Avenue toward our new apartment when I suddenly hear a voice behind me chanting in singsong, "Nyah, nyah, your folks are deaf and dumb, and you all are trash." I turn to see an older boy on a bike. He dismounts, parks it against a fence, and is walking toward me with a menacing look. I don't know what to do, so I continue walking at the same pace, eyes straight ahead, ignoring his talk. When I hear his bike ride away, my body stops shaking.

While Dad and I are drying the Saturday breakfast dishes, I share my frightening experience with him. *"That boy scares me,"* I confess. *"He might be there again on Monday. What shall I do?"* Dad laughs and says, "Think! How can you solve this problem? I know you can find an answer," and he turns to put a pan in the cupboard. He has no more to say on the subject.

After we put the clean dishes in their places, Dad challenges me to a game of chess. We move to the kitchen table, and he sets the board up, reviewing the names of the pieces and their various moves.

Before we start, he warns, "Watch out! *If you are not careful, I will checkmate you! I was high school chess champion at the Illinois School for the Deaf."*

Then he says, *"Chess and checkers increase thinking power because they can train us to think ahead. Ask yourself, 'What will happen if I move here or move there? Should I move two or three spaces in this direction or one space in that direction? Which move will let me win?'"*

"Don't think only of today," he cautions, placing his flat right hand on his nose, the palm touching the tip. "Always be thinking of the future," and, with emphatic movement, he extends that flat hand as far from his nose as possible.

"What you choose today determines what will happen to you tomorrow. Don't let others lead you down wrong paths. Think for yourself." He smiles. *"I think of YOUR*

future often, and I am working hard to make sure you will go to college. Maybe you will work with the Deaf."

I don't win the chess game, but Dad showed me some good moves. To distract me from losing, he jokes, "How do I win an argument with Mother at night?" I shrug my shoulders and give a puzzled look. With a wide grin, he says, "I turn off the light!" and we chuckle. Dad ends our session with, *"I love you SO much,"* his arms drawn open wide to emphasize the "SO." As his twinkling eyes meet mine, I feel his love radiate through my being. I love him dearly, too...

In spite of Dad's distractions, I follow his advice, and I think about that mean boy all day Sunday. By evening, I have a plan, and I know what I will do. Sure enough, after school on Monday, when the crossing guard helps me cross Route 380, I see that boy up ahead, waiting for me on the corner of Frankstown Avenue. So, when I reach Conemaugh Street, I turn quickly, run as fast as I can to Gramma's house, and slip through the back alleys to our apartment.

Hurrah! I avoided that mean boy, and, better yet, I thought of this plan all by myself.

When I tell Mother about it, she seems concerned and says, "I hope that boy won't bother you again." When I tell Dad, he gives me a hug and says, *"That was good thinking and an excellent plan. I am very proud of you."*

On Tuesday Mr. Brown, our principal, says, "I have a job for you, Ruth Ann. At the start of school each morning when we all gather in the big gym, and right after we say our pledge to the flag, I want you to read a short Bible passage aloud into the microphone."

I gulp in surprise! "Don't worry," he says, "I will tell you the Scripture in advance so you can practice." I'm still feeling confident, so I say, "All right, I will try my best." He says, "Good," and he gives me a slip of paper. On it is written, "Psalm 19:1-4." Then he says, "This is what you are to read tomorrow."

When I tell my parents about my new responsibility, Mother says, "Mr. Brown probably chose you because you are a good reader," and Dad says, *"Congratulations, that is a great honor. I am sure you will do a good job."*

I really don't know why Mr. Brown chose me, but my voicing with expression, just as Mother taught me, may have something to do with it. Besides, I'm used to reading the Bible aloud in Sunday school, so that will help me, too...

With Scripture practice added to my homework, I've had very little spare time this week, so my aunts have taken me to the local swimming pool after Sunday dinner. When they spread their towels on the grass to sunbathe, I ask, "May I please go to the pool?" Aunt Millie says, "All right, but, since you can't swim, you must promise to stay in the shallow end of the pool." And, pointing to a high figure in the distance, Aunt Toni adds, "See that man? That's the lifeguard, stay close to him." I promise to do as they directed, and, squinting into the sunshine, I start walking toward that high shape.

Reaching the pool's edge at the lifeguard's perch, I discover that his chair is supported by four tall metal stilts. When I look up, I can see the underside of the man's chin as he scans the wide expanse of water. My ears ring with the crowd's loud screaming and laughter, but no swimmers are in this shallow area. I have it all to myself.

I grab one of the steel legs and slowly ease myself into the cool water until my feet touch the rough cement floor. Carefully inching away from the safety of the pool's rim, I feel the floor gradually slant, slowly bringing me to rising water levels. With each step, the water rises a little until it reaches my shoulders.

I decide to take one more step forward, and, with that step, the pool's floor disappears, and I'm thrashing in panic. Water rushes into my nose and mouth as I sputter, thrash, and bob like a cork. Each time I pop above the water, I try to call "Help!" Instead, I gulp a mouthful of water and sink again. And, all the while, the lifeguard keeps looking outward!

Finally, I'm exhausted, and I have no strength to struggle any longer. But, as my body goes limp, Dad's advice flashes to my mind: *"Think!"* and it comes to me. I'll sink to the bottom of the pool and crawl, feeling my way up the slanted floor to shallow water. Following this plan, I soon stand up, wade to the side of the pool, and climb out. My heart is pounding as I sit on the pool's rim, shivering and trying to catch my breath. I'm feeling numb and disoriented.

When I feel better, I walk back to join my aunts. "Why are you back so soon?" Aunt Toni asks. I casually spread my towel beside hers and reply, "The pool is very crowded." Well, it's the truth! If I tell my aunts the whole story, they might not bring me here again. As I lie down to soak up the sun, I think, *"Thanks, Dad, your advice saved my life."*...

Miss McKeon teaches fourth grade arithmetic. Tall, with flaming red hair, she has a commanding figure that towers over us kids. The class is working on the multiplication tables, and we sometimes play a game to help us learn them. In fact, we are playing it today. I don't like the game.

Miss McKeon writes a multiplication problem on the chalkboard, "4 x 6 =?" Then, she whirls around, snaps her fingers, and points to a startled David in the first row. His face is red as he stutters, "f-f-f-fif-teen?" "WRONG!" bellows Miss McKeon, and, waving her wooden ruler, she orders, "Show me your right hand, palm up!" David starts to sniffle as he obeys. Miss McKeon raises her ruler, and, with gusto, she hits David's palm, WHACK! With scorn, she orders him to sit down and hollers to the class, "FOUR TIMES SIX EQUALS TWENTY-FOUR! Say it with me!" We chant in unison, just as she orders.

Miss McKeon writes a new problem on the board and points to a cringing student. He gives the wrong answer, and another WHACK echoes around the classroom. I am so terrified of Miss McKeon that I sometimes can't think straight. When we play this game, my only thought is, "I hope my teacher won't call on me." So far, she hasn't. I know I'm not sure of the multiplication tables, but I solve my arithmetic problems correctly by counting on my fingers.

Its April, we are still playing the whacking game in Miss McKeon's class, and today she whacked ME! I decide to walk to Gramma's house after school to show her the red and swollen palm of my right hand.

"Miss McKeon hit me," I complain.

"Why sheea do dat?"

"Because I didn't know the right answer."

"It'sa betta you study mo," Gramma says as she applies ice to my palm. When my hand feels better, she says, "You goa now, your mamma, she'sa be hoema soon," and she waves goodbye to me as I sullenly trudge through the alley to our apartment.

By the time Mother gets home from work, my hand is no longer red, so, when I tell her about the day's events, she doesn't seem alarmed. Like Gramma, she definitely does not offer sympathy.

"Maybe you need to work longer on memorizing the times tables," she points out.

"I will try harder," I say. In my heart, I know very well that she is right.

I'm helping Gramma in the kitchen this Sunday when I overhear my name spoken in the distance. I follow the voice to the porch, but I stop just inside the front screen door to eavesdrop. Aunt Millie and Aunt Mary are on the swing, and Aunt Millie is talking.

"And, right after Ruth Ann left for home, Mum grabbed the butcher knife and walked to the school. Finding Miss McKeon sitting at the desk in her empty classroom, Mum waved the knife at her and said, 'What's the matter with you? You beat the kids! If you touch my granddaughter, Ruth Ann, again, I'll kill you.' Then she marched out of the room." My aunts erupt in uproarious laughter while I retreat in panic and fright.

I can't believe Gramma did that, and I dread going to school tomorrow. What will Miss McKeon say? What will Mr. Brown do? I wait for my parents or someone in the family to speak of it, but they say nothing, and no one at school mentions it either.

I am shocked by Gramma's outspokenness, but of one thing I am sure: when it involves defending her family, Gramma is tough...

Soon Mother and Dad receive a letter from Miss Holly, my homeroom teacher. Dad shows it to me, and I read: "Dear Mr. and Mrs. Hazel: Please meet with me in Room 106 on Tuesday afternoon at three."

He looks at me questioningly. *"What do you think your teacher wants to talk about?"* I shrug my shoulders, for I have no idea what Miss Holly wants to discuss— unless it's Gramma's caper. I shudder at the thought.

Mother must work, but Dad and I are seated beside Miss Holly's desk. She talks to Dad as I interpret. "Miss McKeon recommends that Ruth Ann repeat fourth grade because she doesn't know her multiplication tables." I'm disheartened and blushing with shame.

"Mr. Hazel," she continues, "would you be willing to work with Ruth Ann and help her memorize the multiplication tables?" Dad nods yes and ventures to speak to her. "Yes, I will," he replies.

So Dad and I practice diligently until I master the multiplication tables. No longer does Miss McKeon intimidate me.

Nearing the end of fourth grade, Mother and Dad get another invitation to meet with Miss Holly after school, and off I go with Dad. She greets us and says, "Thank you, Mr. Hazel, for practicing the multiplication tables with Ruth Ann. Since she now has them memorized, Miss McKeon has no argument, and I am able to move forward with my plan. I have arranged for Ruth Ann to be double promoted, skipping fifth grade."

I'm astonished at this news, but I don't have time to digest it, for I must keep interpreting for Miss Holly and for Dad.

She continues. "This was possible only with your help, Mr. Hazel, and I applaud you and your wife for the excellent job you are doing in raising your daughter."

I voice for Dad as he replies, *"Thank you for all you did for Ruth Ann, we are grateful."* Words referring to me always sound strange coming from my mouth.

I can't wait to tell Mother the wonderful news: I will be in sixth grade next year.

Chapter 4

MILESTONES

My sixth grade school year is about to end, and all students who will graduate in June are attending an assembly today where awards will be given for the sixth grade honor roll and for sports achievements.

I'm sitting next to my best friend, Sue Pippin. All through elementary school, she and I took turns being first and second on the school's weekly honor roll, and, in sports, we were always on competing teams. She and I are good-natured about our rivalry, so we are sitting beside each other in the crowded auditorium, eager to learn which of us has been first on the honor roll the most times this year. In fact, all of our schoolmates have been trying to guess which of us will be the winner. Everyone is waiting with bated breath.

Mr. Brown announces, "The first place winner for honor roll is Sue Pippin." I am devastated! Nevertheless, I clap and smile as Sue walks to Mr. Brown, accepts her certificate, and returns to her seat, beaming. Suppressing my disappointment, I sincerely congratulate her with a hug.

Next, Mr. Brown declares, "The second place winner is Ruth Ann Hazel." Forcing a smile, I walk to accept my second place certificate. As our principal hands it to me, he announces with loud enthusiasm, "And Ruth Ann gets a special award for being chosen as the best all-around athlete."

I am baffled. Peering at my certificate closely, I see a small round button pinned in its corner, and on the button is an image of a bare foot with wings. Mr. Brown unfastens the button, pins it on my collar, and shakes my hand, saying, "Congratulations, Ruth Ann, for winning TWO awards!" Suddenly I am no longer disappointed, and I remember one of Dad's favorite sayings: "Life is funny that way!" I walk back to my seat, Sue rises to congratulate me, and we hug each other to the sound of widespread applause.

After the ceremony, Mr. Brown announces that all sixth graders will attend Baxter Junior High School for seventh grade, and my classmates and I join in a wild cheer that rings from the rafters.

Before school starts, my parents buy a row house like Gramma's, just one block from my school. The address is 822 Durango Way, Pittsburgh, Pennsylvania...

"Let's celebrate owning our first house by having lunch at a restaurant," Dad suggests. Mother and I are surprised and delighted, for this will be an unusual treat. We seldom eat out, and, when we do, we always eat in a cafeteria.

The restaurant is crowded, and we are standing in a long line waiting to be seated. People push and shove, and, somehow, I am separated from Mother and Dad. They didn't notice that I'm stuck back here, but I'm not worried. I catch glimpses of them as they move up

Ruth Ann and Cousins at the Row House

toward the head of the line. When they're first, I will politely nudge my way through the line to reach them.

Suddenly, I hear a siren in the distance, the sound rapidly coming closer until a vehicle screeches to a stop at the restaurant entrance. From behind us, a booming voice commands, "STEP ASIDE, FOLKS, THIS IS AN EMERGENCY!"

I move to the side with all the others and glance at Mother and Dad. Oh, NO! They are still in place, facing forward! Of course they didn't hear the command, and they're completely unaware of what is happening behind them. They are standing motionless.

I desperately start forward to alert them, but, before I can take one step, a man wearing a uniform brushes past me and reaches my parents first. He roughly shoves them aside and shouts at them in an angry voice, "ARE YOU DEAF, OR ARE YOU JUST DUMB?"

Mother and Dad stumble sideways and have regained their balance when I reach them. Stunned and confused, they look at me questioningly. I am furious at the way that man treated my parents, and I am embarrassed by all the people gaping at us. They probably think my folks are crude and unfeeling.

We step back into place, and I'm explaining the situation to Mother and Dad and hoping that, when people notice me signing, they will realize that my folks are Deaf and will know the reason why they didn't move aside.

My parents now understand the commotion, and they sign to me, *"Sorry for the confusion."* I can't bring myself to tell them about the insult the man flung at them. He already hurt my feelings, so why should I allow him to hurt theirs, too?

At our turn, we follow the waitress to our table amid the stares of diners. I'm not hungry anymore, and I have lost my festive outlook. When our order is delivered, I nibble on my food and try to be cheerful, but, inside, I am still fuming.

Mother and Dad seem not to notice because they are excitedly discussing our moving plans and enjoying our celebration meal. It puzzles me that I see no trace of annoyance on their faces. I do remember when Dad told me not to be angry about mistreatment, but this involved physical abuse!

I am realizing anew that deafness is not only a disadvantage, it sometimes can be dangerous. Without being able to clearly see what is happening around them, people who are deaf can be easy victims of happenstance...

Dad is working overtime on this Saturday, and Mother and I are here at home. She gathers our soiled clothing, the sheets, and the towels, and announces, "I'm going down to the basement to do the laundry." I jump up with anticipation.

"May I come down and watch you? Please?" I beg. *"I like to see the steam rising from the boiling water when you starch Dad's dress shirts."*

"All right, you may watch me, but you must sit high up on the steps. If you get too close to that steam, you might get burned."

I settle partway down and watch through the railing posts. From here, I can see everything clearly. There it is! Steam from the big metal tub is swirling around Mother's head as she stirs the shirts in the hot mixture with a long stick.

Suddenly, Mother's legs buckle, and she collapses. Her stick flies through the air, bouncing and crashing to the cement floor. In one leap, I sail over the remaining steps and run to her. I pull and push to help her sit up, but she is too heavy for me. Her eyes are partly closed, and, with a weak voice, she says, "Go get Gramma, and tell her I need help. Run fast." I nod yes, and, leaving her in place, I spin around, bound up the stairs, burst out the back door, and take off running as fast as I can.

Gramma's house is so far away. Dad once said it's over a mile from our house. With every fiber of my being, I am pressing forward, running as if I'm in a race. I feel like my heart will burst, but I will not stop. People are looking at me with curiosity, and they move apart on the sidewalk to let me speed by.

Finally, I'm in Gramma's backyard, but, when I try to climb the steps, I stumble at the bottom and land on my stomach. My heart is beating wildly. With a trace of strength, I raise my head and call, "Gramma!"

She must hear the panic in my voice because she rushes out onto the back porch with my aunts following. "What'sa matta you?" she shouts in alarm.

"My---mother---fell---in---the---basement," I gasp. "She---sent---me---to---call---you.--She---needs---help." That's all I can muster, for my breath and energy are spent, and my body is completely limp.

One by one, my aunts and Gramma fly down the steps, and I feel the "swish" of their feet as they rush past me. Then silence. I'm left behind!

After I catch my breath and gather strength, I start back home. Far ahead I see Aunt Toni and Aunt Millie running, with Gramma hurrying close behind. I'm at least two blocks away from them, dodging walkers who stare at me with curiosity.

When I arrive home, I discover that Aunt Millie and Aunt Toni have moved Mother to the steps of our front porch, one aunt on each side, holding her up. She is frantically gasping for breath, her lips are blue, and her pale face shows panic and desperation. I am horrified! Something terrible is happening to Mother!

At that very moment, an ambulance pulls up, its red lights flashing, and two men get out. They roll a white cot to the porch, lift Mother, and lay her on it. Then they slide the cot into the back of the van, close the double doors, and speed away with red lights blinking and siren piercing the quiet of the neighborhood. The ambulance is gone just as quickly as it appeared, staring neighbors go back inside their homes, and here I stand, wondering if my mother is going to die.

After the ambulance pulls away, Aunt Toni turns to Gramma and Aunt Millie and says, "Let's go inside and wait until Ed gets home so we can tell him what happened."

As I follow the three into our living room, they start speaking in Italian. Now I know! They don't want me to understand what they're saying because Mother IS going to die. They're waiting for Dad to tell me.

I sit on the sofa feeling alone and scared until I remember: Jesus is with me! Sensing His presence, I am comforted, and my anxiety subsides.

Soon I hear Dad at the back door, and I listen as Aunt Toni tells him what happened. Then he comes to me, puts his arm around my shoulder, and explains.

"Don't worry, Mother will be all right, the doctors know how to help her."

"What is wrong with her?"

"Carbon monoxide gas leaked from the basement hot water heater. Mother breathed the gas, and it made her sick, but you were high up on the stairs, so the spreading gas didn't have time to reach you. Mother is lucky you were there to run for help."

Mother is soon home from the hospital and back to work, and a scary thought keeps nagging me.

What if I had not run fast enough to get help to Mother in time?...

Because Baxter Junior High School is far from Gramma's, I won't be going to her house for lunch, I will eat at school. Mother explains the new routine: "I will tape the door key inside the lid of your lunchbox, and, when it's time for you to leave for school, lock the door from the inside, slam it shut behind you, and try to open it to make sure it's locked." Dad adds, "And, when you get home from school, first finish your homework. Then, if there is time, you may listen to your radio."

School begins, and, at the end of the first week, I arrive home to find a surprise. An old upright piano is in the living room! When Mother gets home, she explains. "One of Aunt Millie's friends gave her old piano to you, and she offered to give you free piano lessons, too." A piano? And lessons? I can hardly believe this. Maybe I can learn to play the piano as well as Mrs. Baker.

I enjoy my piano lessons, and I like my teacher. While I'm practicing my lesson at the piano today,

Dad appears. He watches me for a while and then walks over, puts his left hand on the piano to feel the vibrations, and, with a comical look on his face, he rolls his eyes and sways his hips to the beat as he conducts the song with his right index finger.

"Daddy, you are so silly," I giggle, and I tell him, *"I can't wait until Sunday. Mrs. Baker is going to let me play a song on the piano while we all sing."* Dad smiles and says, "Wonderful! I'm happy for you."

Suddenly, I am sorry that he can't enjoy music...

On Monday morning, I finish dressing for school and start to run down the stairs for breakfast when I get another surprise. I slip at the top and bounce down the stairs on my back with a loud clatter. Each bare wooden step deals a blow to my ribs, and I land in a heap, dazed. I can't breathe! I can't move!

Mother and Dad are in the kitchen having breakfast. They have neither heard the noise nor felt the vibrations of my fall, so no one comes to investigate. I lie there with my cheek resting on the cold linoleum floor, trying to catch my breath and listening for a sound--any sound--that might mean Mother or Dad is coming to call me to breakfast.

At last I hear a chair scrape the floor, and Dad's heavy footsteps are coming in my direction. His shoes stop beside me, and I anticipate the feel of his strong hands, lifting me.

Oh, NO! His shoe is nudging my ribs, and he cries out teasingly, "Ha, Ha, you can't fool me." I can't believe this! With a struggle, I manage to sign, *"I fell."*

My gasps and the panic in my face startle him, and his smile disappears.

Carefully picking me up, Dad carries me into the living room and lays me on the couch. He's holding my hand, and, with a look of deep regret, he says, "I'm sorry, Ruth Ann, I didn't realize you fell down the steps, I thought you were playing games." Weakly, I sign, *"I understand."*

Mother comes into the room, and Dad tells her what happened. They calmly check me for abrasions or broken bones, and, finding none, they sit with me until my breathing returns to normal. *"I feel O-K now,"* I assure them, and I get up, gobble my breakfast, and hurry to school.

On the way, self-pity stirs, but I dismiss it. I can almost hear Gramma saying, "Summa tings we cannota change." And I recall the words of a hymn I learned in Sunday school: "Whatever my lot, Thou hast taught me to say, It is well with my soul." That's Mother and Dad's attitude, and now it is mine.

I signed up for girls' sports and afterschool activities, so I'm arriving home later than usual. Mother says, "You needn't help with dinner and the dishes any longer. It will be best if you spend your time practicing piano and doing your homework." Her news is a welcome surprise, and I thank her for that extra time.

My weekdays are busy with classes, piano practice, homework, and sports, and there is no time for school friends. Nevertheless, I enjoy weekends. On Saturdays, Mother, Dad, and I do our household chores, in the afternoons, we visit Deaf friends, and, in the evenings, we go to the Club. On Sundays, I enjoy Sunday school and dinner at Gramma's.

Often, after we finish eating, I spend time with Aunt Toni. We sit on the swing together, and she tells me about the latest movies, fads, and trends in the Hearing World, a perspective I don't often get at home.

She answers my questions about changes I see in my body and about boys, too. It's our private "girl talk." I go to Aunt Toni for advice on many subjects and have come to realize that she is like my big sister.

I am happy and content with my life.

II
SOJOURNING
1945-1985

"But when I became an adult,
I set aside childish ways."

1 Corinthians 13:11b, NET

Chapter 5

INSIGHTS

B etween 1945 and 1985, the Hearing World sees changes: the civil rights movement is gaining, network television begins, cellular phones and fax machines are popular, and the Apple I home computer is on the market.

In the Deaf World, American Sign Language (ASL) is declared a true language, the Registry of Interpreters for the Deaf (RID) is well-established, closed captioned TV programs are common, the Telecommunication Device for the Deaf (TDD) gives access to the telephone, and Telephone Relay Services (TRS) are in use.

Those years brought transformations in my life. First, I began to mature, with the typical growth spurt shaping my body while my ways of thinking and speaking began to change. I was growing in knowledge and understanding. After suffering with Mother and Dad through the humiliation and the discrimination they endured, any softness I may have had was now turning into inner strength. Aunt Toni and I discussed the change.

"Ruth Ann, you are very mature for your age."

"Yes, I guess I am, and I feel like I am both Hearing and Deaf, like a frog that hops back and forth between land and water, at ease in both worlds."

I joined her in a laugh, knowing full well she couldn't possibly understand my feeling, for how can I explain it clearly if I don't fully grasp it myself? All I know is that I feel different from everyone, both Hearing and Deaf, because I seem to have a double nature.

Then, Dad announced startling news: *"I have accepted a job in the printing department of the University of Chicago Press (the Press). We will move to Chicago in June after you finish seventh grade."*

I was upset. *"Must we move? You already have a good job here. Besides, I will miss Sue, and my teachers, and Gramma, and my aunts, and my friends at the Club. I will miss Sunday school, too."*

Mother and Dad were sympathetic but firm. Dad said, *"We understand how you feel, Ruth Ann, but this move is best for our future."* In a vague way, I understood, but it was not in the realm of my thinking to live away from Mother's family—my family. I clung fast to denial, believing something would surely interrupt Mother and Dad's plans

But my disbelief was short-lived, however, when Mother announced the news at Gramma's on Sunday. Everyone was shocked, and they wished us well, but my eyes were on Gramma, Aunt Millie, and Aunt Toni. They looked stunned and said nothing. They would surely miss me, but how could I ever get along without them? One of Dad's adages came to mind: "Cheer up, the worst is yet to come." It reminded me that, in view of one's entire lifetime, this change was a relatively minor event. I kept that uppermost in my mind as we pursued our plans...

By May 1945, we were packed and ready, but there was one month of school left before I completed seventh grade, so Dad said, *"I think it is best that I travel to Chicago ahead of you and Mother. I will find a place for us to live, and it will be ready when you arrive in June."* He packed his needs and left the next day.

On Sunday, when Aunt Toni and I were chatting, I confided in her. "I'm looking forward to new adventures in Chicago, but I'm unhappy about leaving Gramma, Aunt Millie, and you."

She put her arm around me and said, "I asked your mom if I can travel with you and then stay a week to help you adjust. She likes the idea. Is it OK with you?"

"It's a wonderful idea!" I cried. "Oh, yes, please come with us," and we hugged each other tightly.

Meanwhile, Dad notified us that he found a small apartment on the second floor of a home on Eggleston Avenue at 120th Street in the West Pullman section of Chicago. He signed the rental agreement, and everything was prepared, awaiting our arrival. In just a few more days, we would be on the train. The winds of change were awaiting me in the "Windy City"...

When Mother, Aunt Toni, and I arrived in Chicago, Dad excitedly announced that he wanted me to attend a small private school in the fall, the University of Chicago Laboratory School. *"I have already signed you up to take the entrance examinations,"* he said, *"and, if you are accepted, you will be enrolled in the eighth grade there. You will ride the Illinois Central Electric train (the IC) to attend classes, about an hour's travel each way."*

I interrupted him. *"I would rather attend public school so I can have school friends living nearby,"* but Dad ignored my comment and enthusiastically continued his argument. *"Because I am an employee of the university, you are entitled to a half-tuition scholarship, and, when you pass the entrance tests, the school will award the other half to you. That means you will get an excellent education at no cost to us."*

As usual, Dad expressed every confidence in my abilities, but I was far from convinced. The idea of attending a university school at such a distance was daunting, and I shook my head no. Dad pleaded, *"Please try,"* and Aunt Toni said, "What a great opportunity!" So, even though I doubted I could pass the exams, I humored Dad and agreed to try my best.

I remember very little of those tests. One I especially recall was the Rorschach test. I looked at a series of ink blots and described what I saw in them. I wondered what in the world they were testing, anyway.

To my great surprise and to my parents' delight, I passed those exams and was accepted into the eighth grade at the University of Chicago Laboratory School (Lab). School would start in September, right after my twelfth birthday. I expected it to be a boring summer in the meantime, but that notion quickly vanished.

Soon after Aunt Toni returned to Pittsburgh, she phoned us with sad news: "Grampap had another heart attack, and he died last night." When I told Mother, she looked shocked and exclaimed, "He was only sixty-four!" Then, she focused on practical matters. "Let's pack," she said, "you and I will go to the funeral, but Dad must stay here and work."

Dad deposited us at the train station, and we boarded the overnight coach. Mother let me sit by the window, and, after the conductor dimmed the lights, we adjusted our reclining seats and settled back to sleep. As the train clacked along, I peered into the night at the dark shadowy landscape passing by and lifted my gaze to the brilliant moon lighting the sky.

Memories of Grampap crowded my mind, and a sudden feeling of sadness overcame me. Why hadn't I made an effort to understand my grandfather? Now that opportunity was gone forever. As I scolded myself, I remembered one of Dad's adages: "Never put off until tomorrow, for it may never come." This was a painful lesson in that truth.

We arrived at Gramma's early and found her sitting in her tiny living room surrounded by family. She was weeping, and she rose to meet me with an embrace, bewailing, "He wanna see you, heea loveda you." Her words made no sense to me, for the Bible says love is kind, and Grampap seemed harsh and mean, not only to me, but to others, too. I kissed my beloved Gramma without responding, and Mother and I sat down on the couch beside her.

Arriving at the local funeral parlor, Mother and I walked arm-in-arm to the open casket. As I gazed at

Grampap's body, regret rose to my throat, and I hurried away. Later I admitted to Mother, "It's hard for me to believe that Grampap loved me, and I'm sorry I didn't really know him." In reply, Mother began to recall memories.

"It was difficult for my father to express emotions, and he never tried to speak to me; he didn't know how. There was an invisible barrier between us."

"On the day I was graduating from the Western Pennsylvania School for the Deaf, I was astonished to see my father in the audience. I didn't expect him, for he never showed any interest in me or in my school activities. When the ceremony ended, I looked for him in the crowd, but he was not there."

"Thinking he might have gone to my dorm room, I hurried there, but the room was empty. Then I spied a beautiful bouquet of flowers on the dresser with a lovely greeting card propped up beside it. The card was signed with my father's familiar scrawl."

Rare tears came to Mother's eyes as she admitted, "Like you, I regret I did not know him."

As I sat beside Mother on the train ride to Chicago, I pondered how unhappy I would be never to know my own father, and I shuddered at the thought. My own dear Daddy was my beloved friend and counselor, the foundation of my life.

A feeling of sympathy for Mother stirred within me, and I suddenly realized that she, too, did not openly express her emotions. She was like her father!...

Grampap and Ruth Ann 1937

Once back in Chicago, Mother and I had just finished arranging the apartment when Dad announced, *"I have the address of the Chicago Club of the Deaf in the Loop. Let's start going there on Saturday nights."* That sounded good to me, for I had nothing else to do until school started. We found the place and soon felt at home with our new Deaf family.

At a membership meeting early in July, the president of the Club announced, *"The manager of the Cincinnati Reds baseball team contacted me and asked if the Club would provide a sign language interpreter for*

an upcoming Reds game with the Chicago Cubs at
Wrigley Field. One of the Reds' players, Dick Sipek,
is Deaf, and he will be recognized at that game with
a special presentation."

The members immediately pointed to me. "Rooth,
Rooth," some chanted, while others pointed to me
with one hand and held the other hand high in
the air, fingerspelling *"R-u-t-h-A-n-n,"* over and over
again. I felt a shiver, but I sat quietly. Someone made
a motion to ask me to do the job, the motion was
seconded, there was no discussion, and it passed by
unanimous vote. I didn't stir; I think I was paralyzed
with fright.

The president, Mr. Herbst, looked at me. *"All you
have to do is stand in the middle of the stadium and
sign what is said to Dick Sipek. Then, when Mr. Sipek
signs his reply, you become his voice and speak into
a microphone."* I cringed. When Mr. Herbst says, *"All
you have to do,"* he makes it seem so simple, but he
has no idea what interpreting involves. Thankfully,
Dad stood up and signed to the president, *"Irene and
I will discuss this with Ruth Ann, and we will tell you
our decision at next Saturday's meeting."*

When we got home, I was ready to assert myself
for the first time. I angrily addressed my parents,
shouting and signing, *"NO! I do NOT want to do this.
I've never met Dick Sipek, and I'm afraid I might not
understand his signing. Besides, I DON'T want to
walk out onto that big ballfield."*

"Bah, humbug!" said Dad, waving my argument aside,
"You can do it and do it well." And Mother urged,

"The Club members voted to ask you. They have confidence you can do the job, and so do we. Besides, they said they don't know of anyone else who interprets as well as you do."

I signed and shouted, "IS THAT SO?" While they could not hear the sarcasm in my voice, they would easily recognize it on my face. "You REALLY mean there is NO ONE ELSE TO ASK." With that, I marched to my room, slammed the door, and flopped on my bed.

Sleep didn't come for a long time. I recalled my decision not to disappoint my parents, and I was ashamed of my rebellion. Suddenly, the truth became clear. Like Mr. Herbst, my parents had no idea how difficult interpreting can be. As a matter of fact, how COULD they?

The next day, Mother and Dad came to me, and Dad signed, *"Fear is good when it saves us from danger, but fear is bad when it keeps us away from new experiences that help us learn and grow. Fear tries to trick us and paralyze us, but we must kick it out of our minds, like this."*

He grabbed an imaginary clump of "fear" from his forehead, dropped it toward his right foot, and kicked it up toward the ceiling. Then he smugly dismissed it with a flip of his hand and brushed his palms together to indicate the job was finished. Mother and I joined him in a burst of laughter at his silly antics, and, with resignation, I agreed to do the assignment.

It was Thursday, July 26, 1945, and I couldn't eat much of my breakfast. Mother and I hurried to finish dressing, and she picked out a navy blue dress for me. "Your white arms and hands against a dark background will make it easier for Mr. Sipek to see your signing," she explained. Really? I wondered what color Mr. Sipek would be wearing.

As we took our seats on the streetcar, Dad said, *"Just do your best. Do not think of the people watching and listening, but think only of Mr. Sipek."* And Mother said, "He is depending on you to make everything clear to him, and he trusts you to voice correctly." It occurred to me that Mr. Sipek had no choice but to trust me, and the responsibility weighed heavy.

When we arrived at the stadium, we made our way to our reserved seats at the edge of the field as a voice blared that there were over eleven thousand people in attendance. I squinted up into the sunshine and saw the stands packed with spectators, their clamor filling my ears and vibrating in my head. I shrunk back in my seat. Why did I agree to do this? At 1:45 the game started. Mother and Dad, of course, weren't bothered by the noise, and they were absorbed in the plays, but I had difficulty keeping my mind on the game. I was busy trying to swallow the lump in my throat and to ignore the commotion.

At the time set for the presentation, a man carrying a microphone came out of the dugout, and a small group of men followed after him. When they reached the pitcher's mound, one of the men turned and beckoned toward us. This was it! No turning back! Hang on! As I rose and walked to join the group, I could sense the adrenaline flooding my system. Here

I was, wading into uncharted waters while thousands of people were watching me. Would I drown? When I reached the group of men, one signed, *"Hello,"* and I signed back, *"Hello, M-r S-i-p-e-k."* I faced him with determination, ready for whatever was to follow.

It was easy to sign the presenter's speech, but now I steeled myself to focus on the ballplayer's signs and fingerspelling and to speak his reply clearly into the microphone. I had experience with microphones, but not with public address systems, so what happened next was a total shock.

Mr. Sipek began to sign, and, at the first sound of my voice, I flinched inside as my words BOOMED and ECHOED, seeming to overlap! My heart pounded, and I wanted to flee, but I strained to ignore the echo while I read Mr. Sipek's signs and voiced calmly for him. When the ceremony ended, I nodded goodbye to him and flew back to my seat. I survived!

Mother and Dad welcomed me with a smile, and I suddenly understood. They did not fully share in this occasion, did not see my signing, and did not hear my voice. Yet, in a sense, they were with me through it all, for they equipped me for these times. I was their creation, their pride, and their joy. Surely that knowledge prompted their smiles.

And, just as Dad said, this experience made me learn and grow...

Ruth Ann at Eleven

During that same summer, we met Tom Mayes at the Club. He was a twenty-three-year-old preppy Deaf student working on a graduate degree at the

116

University of Chicago. We took a liking to him, and the feeling was mutual, so there were many Sundays when Tom ate dinner with us, traveling on the IC train from his apartment on the campus to our suburban home. Tom was like Mother in that he spoke so clearly, and with such a pleasant voice, that it was easy for any Hearing person to understand him. We enjoyed chatting about the university and events on campus.

One Sunday, he said, "I think of you as my little sister," and I said, *"That sounds good to me. You can be the brother I've always wanted."* Like Toni, he was older than I by twelve years. I respected Tom for his intelligence and admired his air of self-confidence. I couldn't imagine anything hindering him from a goal he set for himself. He was very young, and he had achieved much. I was curious, so I probed.

"How old were you when you lost your hearing?"

"I was seven and deafened by spinal meningitis, the same disease that got your Mother."

"What was family life for you?"

"Nothing important was ever said in our house."

"Why do you say that?"

A twinkle in Tom's eyes always prepared me for some sort of humor, and he didn't disappoint me.

"Whenever I interrupted a family conversation and asked, 'What are you talking about?' the answer was always the same: 'Nothing important.'" His jesting made it clear that he accepted the situation without anger. I continued to question.

"Where did you go to school?"

"I went through public school and college without an interpreter."

"Really?" I said. Ahh, there was that twinkle again!

"Whenever I walked into a classroom the first time, I always took a seat right beside the prettiest girl and asked her, 'May I please have copies of your class notes?' The girl always said yes."

I chuckled. No doubt Tom's good looks helped in those situations. Sometimes I can still hear Tom talking in earnest. "I have a dream," he is saying. "I want to improve the education of deaf children and to help their parents understand and relate to them. I don't want those children to suffer like I did."

I admired Tom's goals, his vitality, and his spirit. His sense of humor was an asset, too. He often chuckled at the limitations of deafness and enjoyed telling stories on himself. Here is my favorite one.

"I had just purchased a snazzy convertible. The first day I drove it to my office, my coworkers crowded around it, raving with admiration, and I felt proud. At the end of the day, as I drove home, I seemed to catch every red light, and, at every stop, I noticed pedestrians turn to look at my car. By the time I arrived home, my pride had turned into conceit, and I smugly pulled into my driveway. As I was getting out of the car, my neighbor hurried over and said, 'Tom! Your horn is stuck!'"

Tom started bringing his Deaf girlfriend, Julia Burg, to our Sunday dinners. She and I got along famously because we both had the same interest—teaching. Julia spoke as well as Tom. She said she became deaf as a child, went through public school by lipreading, and learned to sign at Gallaudet College.

After he graduated, Tom married Julia, and they moved to Michigan where she became a teacher of the Deaf, and Tom worked toward his goals. Happily, they visited us each summer when they came to Chicago to visit Julia's twin sister, Celia Warshawsky, who was one of my closest Deaf friends.

Tom and Julia were among the Deaf friends with whom I bonded, and my love for them ran deep. Although we kept in touch regularly over the years, none of us could foresee that we would someday live in the same town and work on projects together...

Soon after we moved to Chicago, Mother bargained her way into a job at the Muter Company where they made radio parts on assembly lines. When she indicated on her application that she was Deaf, the owner told her he did not hire handicapped people. Undeterred, Mother said, "I'm willing to work for you for one week without pay, and, at the end of the week, if you are not satisfied with my work, I will leave quietly. But, if you like my work, you can hire me." He accepted her unusual proposal.

At the end of that week, the owner said, "You're hired! You produced more piecework than any other worker on your line. How do you explain that?" Mother replied, "That's easy. Because I'm Deaf, I'm not distracted and slowed by joining the conversations of my coworkers." Not only was Mother a star worker, she earned the respect and admiration of her boss and the other employees, as well.

One day Mother arrived home with this story. "This morning I went to the ladies' room during our work break. When I went to the sink to wash my hands, I first took my wedding rings off and put them in my pocket where I always keep a tissue. After I dried my hands, I pulled the tissue out of my pocket and wiped my brow. At that very moment, a coworker washing her hands at the next sink quickly turned to look at me and then continued her hand washing. I thought it was strange."

"I left the restroom and was walking to my work station when I remembered my rings and reached into my pocket. They were not there! I realized they must have fallen on the floor when I pulled the tissue from my pocket, so I rushed back to the restroom and looked everywhere, but I found no trace of my rings. Then I thought of the woman at the next sink, the only other person in the washroom at that time. Surely she heard my rings fall. I walked straight to her work station."

"I said, 'I think my wedding rings fell out of my pocket in the restroom a few minutes ago, did you hear them fall?' She said she hadn't heard anything like that, but I read her face, and it betrayed her. Now I was positive that this lady had my rings, so I went to my boss and told him my story. I asked him to please talk to the woman and convince her to give my rings back to me, but he said, 'You must be mistaken, Irene, this nice lady surely would not do such a thing. Perhaps your rings fell down the sink drain.' And he declined to do anything about it."

"What are you going to do, Mother?" I asked, and she said, "I'm going to talk to my boss again tomorrow." There were two more "tomorrows" in which Mother confronted her boss and presented her case. On the third day, Mother arrived home wearing her rings!

Smiling triumphantly, Mother explained, "When I arrived at work this morning, I found my rings on my work table. I put them on and continued wearing them as I went on with my work. No one said a word about it to me, so I'll not mention it again. I don't want to embarrass the woman..."

I admired Mother's persistence. As I watched her in action, I soon realized her strength grew out of the devastating blows life had dealt her. First, she was stricken by a disease that abruptly stole her hearing, and, refusing to let that deter her, she worked hard to make the best of her life.

Then, at twenty-four, she met a well-known and respected Deaf gentleman, Edwin M. Hazel, who caught her fancy. He was thirteen years older, stable and secure. They married, and he whisked her off to a distant state to live in his new home. Life was bliss, but, shortly afterward came the unexpected setbacks that left her the sole family breadwinner.

That was yet another misfortune, but Irene faced life with the emotional and physical toughness she already acquired. She labored tirelessly to create a happy family, and she saved every spare penny to reach her goal of owning a nice home someday.

I watched Mother handle her every task with her best effort. Although she worked full time, she served nutritious meals, dressed us in nice clothing, kept an immaculate house, volunteered on many Club projects, and took time to teach signing to me and to hearing folks. She seemed to pack more than twenty-four hours into one day.

Mother expected a lot from me, too. From the time I was five, I set the table, cleared it, dried dishes, made my bed, and dusted all the furniture weekly.

She was all business, and there seemed to be no softness about her. Her rare smile was not made with lips but was shown by the gleam in her eyes accompanied by the crinkles at their corners. I sometimes found it difficult to "read" her face, and her sternness intimidated me. Still, I knew Mother loved me, and I admired her efficiency, her intelligence, and her organization. I did my best to please her.

By the time Mother was in her mid-forties, employers were no longer rejecting disabled workers, and she was able to get a job reconciling checks at the Continental Illinois National Bank in the Chicago Loop, working there until she retired.

Not long after she began working at the bank, Mother remarked, "I finally got a job where I can use my brain..."

Irene S. Hazel 1947

I was twelve and home on spring break from Lab when Dad approached me with a proposal.

"The editor of the Deaf American national magazine invited me to write a monthly parliamentary law column. I want to accept, but I will need your help editing my English. Can you spare the time?"

"Of course I can, but you must teach me the parliamentary words and their meanings, and then show me the signs for them."

Dad agreed, and we enjoyed our editing sessions, often joking about our new dictionary game. Dad's long-running column was a success, and he was recognized in the Deaf community as an expert in parliamentary law. He was present to advise at all NAD conventions.

The vocabulary I learned while we edited turned out to be valuable in 1953 when Dad told me, *"I applied to become a member of the American Institute of Parliamentarians (AIP), and I am scheduled to take a written and an oral exam. Will you interpret for me?"* Of course I said yes.

I didn't know the answers, but I faithfully interpreted using the correct words and signs. Dad passed easily, becoming the first nationally certified Deaf parliamentarian in American history. He was featured in the June 1953 "Silent Worker" magazine and the October 1966 issue of the "Deaf American."

I am proud of my father's accomplishments...

Mother and I were asleep, and Dad was at work late one night when our home phone rang. I was startled to hear Dad's voice! He sounded miserable.

"Ruth Ann, I want you to know I love you, but I must say goodbye." Panic gripped me, and, even though I knew he couldn't hear me or understand me, I shouted into the phone, "Daddy! Daddy! What's wrong? Where are you going?" Silence. He hung up.

I scrambled to find my phone book and dialed the Press' central number, asking to be transferred to the Monotype Department. Bruce, the night supervisor, answered the phone, and I spoke to him with urgency.

"This is Ed Hazel's daughter. He just phoned me, and he sounded very upset. I'm concerned. Please, will you check on him to see if he is all right?"

"Sure, hold on." Bruce spoke casually, but I was tense and waited with misgivings. He returned to say "Your Dad is OK," and he abruptly hung up.

I wasn't satisfied, so I called that department again and asked for Tom, one of Dad's coworkers. When he came to the phone, I described my earlier phone conversations and questioned him.

"Do you know what happened?"

"I certainly do. Bruce is always belittling your dad and constantly finding fault with his work. He refers to Ed as 'the dummy' and makes abusive gestures to him. Tonight he was especially ugly to Ed, and it upset me, too. The fact is, Bruce is jealous of Ed's skill on the machines. Your dad is an expert, and the rest of us in the department admire him greatly."

I thanked Tom for his feedback and hung up. Now I understood! Dad put up with that treatment night after night. No wonder he battled stomach ulcers! My eyes brimmed with tears as I felt his pain, and I recognized that familiar sting of injustice.

I went back to bed. Tossing and turning, I kept looking at the clock, waiting for Dad to come home. At two o'clock, I heard the back door close softly, and I sprang out of bed to meet him. He looked drawn and tired, and his shoulders sagged, but he gave me a hug.

"Daddy, why did you phone me? What happened?"

He avoided my eyes. *"I'm sorry I phoned you. Don't worry, everything is all right. You'd better go back to bed, you need your sleep."*

Then, he walked past me into the kitchen. Obviously, he did not want to talk about it, so I went back to bed.

Inside, I was in turmoil; I felt angry, frustrated, dejected, and sad. I couldn't sleep.

In the morning, I was amazed to see no anger in Dad's face. He clearly had forgiven Bruce—again. Surely, this was the most remarkable of Dad's accomplishments...

I remember the day I was called home when Dad was taken to the hospital by ambulance. We learned that he collapsed because his ulcers were bleeding, and the loss of blood made him weak.

When they discovered Dad was Deaf, most of the hospital staff made little effort to talk to him. I sensed they felt awkward in this unfamiliar situation, so I prepared a sign in large letters—PATIENT IS DEAF —and placed it on the wall above his headboard. Then, I put a notepad and pen on his bedside table to motivate others to converse with him. "Yes, he can read and write," I assured them.

As workers entered the room, I signed their comments to Dad and voiced Dad's replies. I also taught them a few useful signs. Thankfully, most of them were open

Edwin and His AIP Certificate 1953

to learning and seemed fascinated with nonverbal ways of communicating. In addition, Dad's good humor and joking set them at ease.

On the third day, I was sitting at Dad's bedside when a team of doctors swept into the room. They introduced themselves, and one of them said to me, "Please step into the hallway," and he escorted me out. I asked, "What are you going to do?" and he replied, "We're going to put a feeding tube down your father's throat into his stomach." "Please," I begged, "let me stay. I can help convey that to my dad and interpret your directions. That way, he can cooperate." The doctor was curt. "Sorry," he said, "it's against hospital rules." Frustrated, I reluctantly remained in the hall.

I was wringing my hands and anxiously pacing when a nurse came out to say, "Your father is not cooperating, and the doctors want you to come in and help." She didn't have to say that twice! I hurried inside, suppressing the urge to say, "I told you so."

I stood at the foot of Dad's bed, and, when he saw me, his expression changed from bewilderment and fear to relief. I signed as a doctor explained, "We want to put this tube down your throat into your stomach; it will allow your ulcer to heal. Please help by swallowing the tube each time I tell you."

Dad calmly nodded yes and fixed his eyes on me as I signed, *"swallow, swallow, swallow,"* in tandem with the doctor's words. Dad swallowed, and, much to the doctors' surprise, the tube was easily and quickly put into place. I hoped those doctors and nurses learned something that day...

And I remember when Mother was hospitalized after foot surgery. I arrived at her hospital room early one morning to find her frantic. "I'm glad you're here," she cried, "I've needed to use the restroom for over an hour, but no one answers my call button. I have been pressing it repeatedly. Will you please call someone to help me?"

I immediately went to the nearest nurses' station and spoke to the nurse at the desk. "My mother, Irene Hazel, says she has been pressing the call button for over an hour, but no nurse or aide has shown up in her room. She needs help walking to the bathroom."

"Oh!" said the nurse, "I thought she was accidentally touching that button because, every time I replied by intercom, no one answered." I reminded her, "She can't hear you, she's Deaf, remember?" The woman blushed and immediately hurried to Mother's room. But I didn't follow. I waited at her desk for her return.

"Is my mother's chart flagged with a notation that she is Deaf?" I asked. She paused to consider my question. "Well...no...but I think I'll do that. It will alert the nurses on each shift." I grinned. "Good idea," I said, thankful for an iota of progress.

Events like these were no longer upsetting, for I had long observed Mother and Dad accepting them as natural consequences of their deafness. They clung to the belief that the unfavorable treatment from Hearing folks is unintentional and, therefore, is forgivable. Their hope was to educate the public.

They planted that seed in me, and it was sprouting.

Chapter 6

TRANSITION

The summer before my second year at Lab, Mother and Dad bought a newly-built white frame home on a tiny lot at 12024 Wentworth Avenue in West Pullman. A typical Chicago bungalow, it was half a block from the IC tracks, just as our apartment was, but I now had a shorter walk to the train station.

Lab was such an exciting place, nothing like my school experiences so far. All my teachers were creative and made our academic subjects exciting. I enjoyed the extracurricular activities, remaining after school to participate in a few hobby clubs and in sports. I also volunteered to supervise the primary children as they waited for the bus.

My drama teacher, Miss Booth, made a fuss over me. "I love your facial expressions, your gestures, and your body language," she said. "You convey the characters so well." She didn't know that my visual communication with Deaf people had a lot to do with it. With every play, Miss Booth cast me in a leading role—except for one.

For the play, "Little Women," Miss Booth asked me to take a character part, that of Aunt Josephine March, a strict and no-nonsense woman. By opening night, I knew my lines and had practiced facial expression, voice quality, demeanor, and gestures. My costume and jewelry completed my character. This kind of role would be a new experience, and I was excited.

The curtain rose on the scene where I was to scold Jo, the willful sister. Deep into my monologue, I was shaking my finger and scolding when WHOOSH! The bracelet on my wrist went flying, bouncing and rattling across the stage floor and sliding under the edge of a side curtain. Jo and the other characters onstage were stunned, and they immediately froze in their tracks, speechless.

Without a blink and in character, I shrieked at Jo. "WELL, DON'T JUST STAND THERE GAWKING, CHILD. PICK THAT BRACELET UP AND BRING IT TO ME IMMEDIATELY." Jo was shaken out of her stupor and scrambled to obey. I grabbed the bracelet from her with much irritation, put it on my wrist, and continued my dialogue until it ended.

When I exited at the close of that scene, Miss Booth was waiting for me, and she was glowing. "Quick thinking!" she said, "I am so proud of you," and she gave me a bear hug. She didn't know that my interpreting tasks taught me to stay in my role and to think quickly.

With all that stage work, I became well-known and well-liked. To my surprise, I was elected captain of the girls' field hockey team, chosen the leader of the girls' basketball team, and selected to be a cheerleader. These developments changed my perception of myself. I no longer was valued only for serving my parents and their friends in the Deaf World, I now had a brand new self-identity in the Hearing World. To mark the change, I dropped my middle name. Everyone was to call me "Ruth"—except Mother and Dad, of course.

In a tenth grade school-wide election, I was voted Girls' Club president. In that role, I introduced projects, appointed and worked with committees, delegated responsibility, and made impromptu speeches. Every such experience was exhilarating, and my shyness seemed to evaporate into thin air...

Lab didn't offer eleventh and twelfth grades, so we tenth graders were called to a special assembly. Mr. Sands, our principal, explained that, under the Robert Maynard Hutchins plan, each of us had two choices: to attend our local public high school for eleventh and twelfth grades, or to skip eleventh and twelfth grades and go straight to the college as freshmen. "But, if you want to go straight to the college, you must first pass a three hour test in each core subject," he warned.

He explained that those who went straight to the university would receive their high school diplomas at the end of their college sophomore year and their bachelor's degrees at the end of their senior year. I was excited at the prospect, and, when I told Mother and Dad I wanted to take the exams, they approved.

I will never forget the English exam. Each of us received blank sheets of paper upon which we were to write an essay in three hours. The proctor distributed random titles, and, when I got mine, I was shocked: "Marriage and Divorce." At thirteen years of age, I had to do a lot of serious thinking before I began writing that essay, but I did my best.

When I received the test results, I was thrilled to find that I not only passed all the exams, I was excused from taking the mandatory three years of college English! My closest girlfriends also passed the exams, and we excitedly looked forward to being together.

Those long train rides were worth it. If we had stayed in Pittsburgh, I would miss the glorious days at Lab and this great opportunity to enter college early. Thank you, Mother and Dad.

It was June, and college wouldn't start until fall, so I got a full-time summer job in the mail room of the Press. My plan was to pay for my textbooks...

In September I turned fourteen and entered the University of Chicago as a freshman.

As it was at Lab, my parents paid no tuition fees for my four years at the college; the university waived half the tuition because Dad was an employee, and my sorority, Mortar Board, awarded me the other half. What's more, there were no dormitory housing costs since I lived at home. I suspect this was well beyond Dad's expectations. In any case, my folks never could afford to send me to such a great university.

I took the college core classes in the mornings, but, in the afternoons, I worked in the office of the Press using a comptometer to calculate payroll. That left no time for me to take education courses, and the shortage of necessary credits would delay my dream of becoming a teacher. I accepted that reality because my goal was to cover my expenses to a larger extent.

My social life was full. Girls from all walks of life were my sorority sisters, and we performed service projects, dated fraternity fellows, and attended dances. After each evening event, I stayed overnight at a sorority sister's house near the campus to avoid riding the IC alone at night. We girls had plenty of dates and enjoyed comparing notes afterwards.

The boys who dated me had to drive from 59th Street to 120th Street to pick me up, and, when they arrived, I always invited them inside to meet my folks. Invariably, they appeared nervous and awkward when watching us sign. After introductions, they smiled and nodded self-consciously at my folks, then rushed me out the door. Mother, Dad, and I chuckled when recalling such scenes. Poor fellows!

Not long after I began working at the Press, a young man in the Lithography Department caught my attention. He always greeted me as I walked through his section picking up timesheets. Curious, I asked about him and learned his name was Bob Reppert, and he operated a giant camera, the first step in the offset printing process. I also found out that Bob was six years older than I and had been in the Navy.

"I know your dad," Bob called to me one day as I walked through his department. With timesheets in hand, I stopped to ask, "How is that?" He replied, "When I walk out of the Press building at the end of my day, I often meet your father arriving for the night shift. He always smiles and greets me with a salute." "Oh," I said, "that salute means 'Hello.'" To my surprise, Bob smiled and saluted!

"I understand that you live in West Pullman," he continued. "Well, I live in Ivanhoe, not far from there. Would you like a ride home after work today?"

His offer tempted me. I could avoid the long walk down the Midway to the IC station and the boring train ride home. It didn't take me long to decide.

I modestly replied, "Yes, that would be nice." So I rode in his shiny red 1949 Ford convertible, and the ride gave us an opportunity to get acquainted. Bob told me his father was a printer, and we laughed when we realized we had something in common—the printer's ink in our blood. Bob was more mature than the fellows I had been dating, and he had a delightful sense of humor. I enjoyed his company.

Before long, he invited me to go with him on a Saturday night date. "I would like to take you to dinner in the Loop and then to the 'Blue Note' jazz club afterward where the blind pianist, George Shearing, is playing." I accepted.

When Bob picked me up that afternoon, I invited him inside, introduced him in sign to my folks, and then waited, curious for his reaction. Fascinated by our signing, he asked me brightly, "How do you say 'Hello, I'm happy to meet you?'" I interpreted his question, and Mother and Dad demonstrated. When Bob signed the greeting back to them, they were surprised and pleased. And my heart was warmed...

It was early afternoon on Sunday, October 30, 1950 when our doorbell rang, and I opened the door to a beggar wearing a dress and the mask of a woman. "She" was at least five foot ten, and, when she said, "Trick-or-treat," in a falsetto voice, I suspected this was a teenage boy.

"You're much too early for trick-or-treating," I said, "Halloween is tomorrow. Besides, aren't you too old for this sort of thing?" There was no reply, so I snappily said, "I'm sorry, I have no treats for you." I shut the door before another word could be spoken.

An hour later, the doorbell rang again, and, this time, it was Bob. He was wearing blue jeans, and his red convertible was parked at our curb.

"I was in the area, and I thought I'd drop by," he said with a grin that grew into an impish laugh.

"Oh! It was YOU in that costume," I exclaimed, and we laughed together.

Bob said, "I apologize for the trick, let me make it up to you. Come join me for a malted milk treat." I teasingly replied, "That's the least you can do." He drove us to the local Rexall drugstore where we sat at the soda fountain for our treats. My malt was icy cold, but my heart was melting.

Soon Bob invited me to meet his parents at Sunday dinner. I was a bit nervous, but his folks were warm and gracious and set me at ease immediately. They tactfully asked about my background, my folks, and my plans for the future. I learned about them, too. They met at Kansas State Teachers College where his mom taught home economics and his dad taught printing. They married and moved to Chicago where his dad founded the Chicago School of Printing located in the Loop. They had lived in Ivanhoe since the time Bob and his sister were babies. I liked Bob's parents immediately.

Not long after that visit, Bob phoned to tell me his father passed away from a sudden heart attack at age sixty-one. He suffered with a defective heart valve, the result of childhood scarlet fever. I was so fortunate to have had the opportunity to meet him.

When Bob and I drove into the funeral home parking lot, it was overflowing with cars, and he explained that his dad was well-loved by his friends and business associates.

Hmmm. This was true of Bob, too.

Once inside the parlor, I met Bob's older sister, Betty, her husband, Tom, their two boys, and Bob's aunts, uncles, and cousins, too. They were lovely people, and they greeted me warmly. We all agreed that it was too bad our meeting had occurred at such a sad occasion.

When my senior year began, Bob asked me to marry him, and I said yes. So, after dinner at our house one Sunday, while Mother was in the kitchen, Bob gave Dad a note asking for my hand in marriage. Dad read it and happily said, "Yes, if it's OK with Irene, too," and, of course, it was! Even though I was just seventeen and Bob was an "older man" of twenty-three, they didn't hesitate one moment, for Bob had endeared himself to them, as well as to me.

Not long afterward, Bob took me to meet his newlywed friends, Chuck and Gean Krueger. We were in their apartment, playing a card game at their kitchen table, when they commented on my diamond engagement ring. I told them, "I was so excited when I first wore this ring that I kept getting up during the night to look at it."

Bob jokingly added, "...until I hollered, 'WILL YOU PLEASE COME BACK TO BED? THE LIGHT KEEPS WAKING ME UP.'"

We all roared with laughter at this unbelievable and preposterous scenario.

That wisecrack would not be funny nowadays...

Our fall wedding was simple. We reserved Graham Taylor Chapel near the university campus for the afternoon ceremony and the downstairs garden cloisters for the reception. Cake, cookies, punch, coffee, and tea would be served. My white satin dress was semi-formal and of ballerina length, its hem stopped just above my ankle. I paid less than two hundred dollars for the dress, the fingertip veil, and the shoes, and my earnings covered the cost nicely.

A week before the wedding, our Deaf friends, Celia and Lenny Warshawsky, invited us to have lunch with them in their new apartment. Celia had just become the first Deaf public school teacher in Illinois, scheduled to teach deaf and hard of hearing children. We were going to help celebrate her victory.

As it was planned, Gramma, Aunt Millie, and Aunt Toni arrived by car in time to join us for the visit.

We climbed the steps to the Warshawsks' second floor apartment, and, when Celia opened the door, a group of Deaf friends from the Club stood behind her signing, "*Surprise!*" They showered us with many lovely gifts, and, when the party ended, Mother, Dad, Bob, and I left for home. The rest of the family would follow in Aunt Toni's car.

We arrived home to a phone ringing, and it was Aunt Toni. "We're in the hospital emergency room," she said. "Gramma fell down the apartment stairs, and her glasses made a gash near one of her eyes. They're stitching her up now, so we'll be late." I was upset and anxiously waited to see her.

My dear Gramma arrived home with a swollen black eye bordered by stitches and vowed, "I'ma no go to da wedding. People, dey look atta my eye anna nota you." She didn't want to upstage me!

"Oh, please," I cried, "I'll be unhappy if you don't come." But Gramma was determined. Her absence from our wedding is one of my deepest regrets.

The rehearsal dinner was held at our house, and our tiny dining room narrowly seated the bridal party of eight. Just as Bob requested, Gramma and Mother prepared and served his favorite meal, spaghetti and meatballs. But, by the time we all finished eating, Bob had barely taken a bite. "Is something wrong with the spaghetti?" Mother asked him. "No, I just don't feel like eating," he murmured, "it must be nerves." We all howled, and a round of teasing followed. Poor Bob!

No interpreter was found for the wedding, so our Deaf guests took aisle seats for a good view. As we practiced, Dad and I walked down the aisle in step as I pressed his arm in time to the music. When the minister asked, "Who gives this woman...?" I squeezed Dad's arm, and he said as clearly as he could, "Her mother and I do." Then he sat down beside Mother. From that moment on, they and our Deaf friends were excluded from all auditory input. They had to be content with watching the pageantry, staring at our backs, and catching a glimpse of the minister now and then. Their one and only interpreter was busy getting married.

Soon after we returned from our honeymoon, I sent my dress to Gramma's relatives in Italy. They said the town's brides would take turns wearing it. As we mailed the box, Bob joked, "I wonder if the dress will accumulate spaghetti sauce stains."...

We bought a new house in the Ivanhoe section of Riverdale, a fifteen minute drive from my parents' home. So, when our son, James Edwin, and our daughter, Linda Ann, were born, Mother and Dad thrived as grandparents. From the time they sat in high chairs, the kids became Mother's sign language "students," and Dad resumed his teasing and advising. My folks sometimes babysat for us, often ate dinner with us, and always joined us for special family events and holidays. With no way to keep in touch, we communicated through written notes that Dad carried back and forth between us. We always had the option of contacting each other by phone through kind neighbors if that should ever became necessary.

Bob and Ruth, October 4, 1952

I was a stay-at-home mom, determined to be everything to our children that my parents could not be for me. I eagerly read books on parenting, and Dr. Spock's book, "Baby and Child Care," became my guide. Still, I followed my upbringing. I read stories and nursery rhymes aloud as Aunt Millie did, guided, listened, and hugged as Dad did, and, like Mother, I tried to be a good housekeeper. Establishing a household and child rearing definitely were challenging and growing experiences.

Bob was eager to be an attentive parent, too. When our son was two, Bob said, "I think I'll build a fence around our backyard so Jimmy will have a nice safe place to play." We chose a basketweave type of fence, and Bob spent his two-week summer vacation building a fence six feet high. Then, he set up a sandbox and a swing set. We didn't realize that basketweave fences provide easy footing. We had a lot to learn.

The first day I let Jimmy go outside to play, I sat by the kitchen window to watch him. How cute! He was playing in the sandbox and having fun on the swings. The doorbell interrupted me, so I went to answer it. When I returned to the window and looked outside, Jimmy was nowhere to be seen!

I ran outside in a panic, just in time to see a neighbor leading our explorer home. That little rascal greeted me with a cheerful, "Hi, Mommy!" This was a clue about life with Jim: he would be inquisitive, active, and adventuresome—a typical boy.

Our back yard became a popular neighborhood playground, and Bob turned our basement into an inviting playroom equipped with shelves of toys. So, as time went on, I not only cared for Jimmy, I often supervised the neighborhood kids, as well. I enjoyed every minute.

When Linda arrived, we had a docile little girl with bouncy curls, always smiling. When she was a Brownie Girl Scout, I taught the girls in her troop some signing so they could earn badges, but I made them promise they would not use those signs inside their schoolrooms. Linda also was a tomboy, seldom wearing dresses and opting to wear comfortable jeans to tag along with her brother and his friends. I thought she was beautiful, but I didn't want her to know it. I preferred that she focus on other subjects, not on her looks.

One night, when Linda was nearing four, I sat on the edge of her bed to tuck her in, just as I always did for both children. As I hugged her, I whispered in her ear.

"When I was a little girl, I used to dream of the sweet daughter I would have some day, and, honey, you are far more wonderful than I expected."

She whispered back, "Mommy, you're better than I expected, too." I stifled my laugh.

For Bob, his family always came first. He taught Linda and Jim to handle tools to make minor repairs, and he supported their every interest. He and Jim were active in Boy Scouts and in the Adventure Guides, a Young Men's Christian Association (YMCA) father-and-son organization, establishing a strong peer group for Jim. Bob also introduced us to nature, pointing out every bird, butterfly, and crawling creature.

I often was a room mother at school, Bob and I team taught our kids' Sunday school classes, and we were counselors for the church youth group when Jim and Linda were members. We chaperoned teenagers on planning retreats, and teens came and went in our basement recreation room where the refrigerator was always stocked with soft drinks.

Late one afternoon, when the kids were about eight and ten, I was preparing supper when I heard screams from the front yard, and I hurried outside to find what the commotion was all about. "Mom, look! Dad caught a bat," Jim hollered. Bob smiled triumphantly as he quickly placed a wood plank over our discarded aquarium. Inside was a bat hanging upside down on a branch taken from a nearby bush. Well, I certainly didn't expect what happened next.

Everyone came inside for supper, including the bat! Bob set the aquarium beside the table, and we studied that bat while we ate. "This is cool," chirped Jim, and Linda stared in awe, but I was repulsed by the creature. I kept my eyes on my plate and endured the biology lesson.

From the time they both were small, I took Jim and Linda for a weekly swimming lesson at the YMCA in the nearby town of Harvey. It was a valuable opportunity that I never had. And, when they were older, we frequented the YMCA family camp in Dolton where there was a sizeable swimming pool to enjoy all summer. Eventually, I did learn to swim, but I had no stamina to endure for long. A remnant of fear hindered me. Nevertheless, I did acquire enough skill to avoid drowning!

Thanks to Bob, we became a camping and fishing family, complete with a three-room tent and a boat, and our annual summer vacations found us tenting, fishing, and waterskiing in Ontario, Canada. Jim and Linda soon were skilled at outdoor living and became keen animal lovers and birdwatchers. Much too soon, and before we knew it, they were attending the University of Illinois at Urbana-Champaign.

Jim has a Bachelor of Science degree with a major in psychology and a Master of Theology degree majoring in pastoral leadership. When he is not pastoring, he is an artisan of wall coverings.

Linda has a Bachelor of Science degree in education and a Bachelor of Fine Arts degree. She did her student teaching in Celia's class. Formerly head of the Preschool Department of the South Carolina School for the Deaf, Linda currently is a nationally certified sign language interpreter and a visual artist...

Linda and Jim 1976

Although I immersed myself in my roles as wife and mother, I held fast to the Deaf World through my parents and our closest Deaf friends. This kept my "Deaf self" on life support. But, a few times, when Mother relayed a request from a friend asking for my interpreting services, I easily declined, for I finally could say no. I definitely had my fill of interpreting in childhood.

Meanwhile, I followed my dream of becoming a teacher. During our children's preschool years, Bob babysat one night a week while I took education courses at Lewis College and Chicago Teachers College. By the time Linda started kindergarten in 1961, I had my certificate in hand and began my teaching career. Both children attended Roosevelt School while I taught at Lincoln School. Both schools are in the Chicago suburb of Dolton, District 148.

One nice bonus of my teaching career was the fact that it freed me to be home with our children during summer vacations. I think Dad recognized this practicality, and perhaps that was the reason he never again mentioned my working with the Deaf.

I taught for twenty-four years, most of them in kindergarten, and, as my teachers at Lab did, I made learning fun. For example, I taught phonics— the sounds of speech—using the Goldman-Lynch reading program featuring the puppet, High Hat, who charmed my students with games and songs. They easily and quickly learned to read before moving on to first grade.

I often thought about how difficult it must surely be for a deaf child to learn to read without being able to hear the sounds of the alphabet letters.

Each year I told my students about my parents and our Deaf friends and taught them a few signs, like *"stop," "sit," "stand," "quiet,"* and *"line up."* They were proud of our silent signals and competed to be first to follow my signed commands. During school assemblies, they quietly obeyed while noisy students in other classes stared with curiosity at my motions.

Late one September, after school was dismissed, my principal, Mr. Bush, came to my room. "Mrs. Reppert," he said, "a boy in one of the district kindergartens is having trouble adjusting. He is rebellious in class, and his Deaf parents say that he refuses to sign with them in public. When I heard about the situation, I told the principal, 'I'm sure Mrs. Reppert can handle him.'" He grinned sheepishly.

"May we transfer him to your class?"

"Of course you can. I can definitely relate to this child, so I'm willing to try to help him."

"I knew you would accept him. His name is Carl Harmon. I will bring him to your class next week."

Before Carl arrived, I met with Mr. and Mrs. Harmon in my classroom, and they were thrilled to learn that I signed and that my parents were Deaf. They asked, *"Can you help our boy?"*

I answered, *"I will try my best, but I need your help. Can you come again after school next Friday?"*

"Carl and I will wait for you, and we will talk about our classroom activities. I want him to watch us, and, hopefully, sign with us, too." They excitedly agreed to meet with us at three o'clock sharp.

On Monday, Mr. Bush quietly ushered Carl into my room and left. My students were sitting at their tables in the middle of a lesson, and I didn't want to interrupt them, so I beckoned for Carl to sit in a chair at a table, intending to give him some lesson material. He scowled at me, stood determined, and shook his head no. I ignored him and continued with the class. Soon Carl was wandering around the classroom inspecting the interest centers and the toy drawers. While the class kept working, I went to him and spoke quietly.

"Carl, I'm your new teacher, Mrs. Reppert, welcome to my class. It looks like you don't want to sit in your chair, is that right?" He nodded yes, crossed his arms, and glared defiantly, but I politely continued.

"Well, since you don't need your chair, I will put it in my closet. When you are ready to sit in it, let me know, and I'll put it back at the table for you." Carl looked disappointed at having missed a quarrel.

The children and I moved on to another project, and we were having fun when Carl called out, "Teacher, can I have my chair now? I want to play, too."

"Yes, you may," I said casually, retrieving his chair. I put it at the table, and, when Carl willingly sat down, I introduced him. "Children, this is your new classmate, Carl Harmon. His parents are Deaf, like mine." The boy looked at me in surprise as one of the children cried out, "He knows sign language! He's a lucky duck."

I asked the children, "Would you like to learn some new signs?" and, in unison, they enthusiastically cried, "Yes," so I turned to Carl. "Will you please teach your new friends some signs?" He hesitated, then nodded yes, so I suggested, "How about teaching them, 'Please' and 'Thank you?'" Carl showed the signs, and his classmates eagerly copied him. "Let's use those signs every day," I suggested.

My meeting with Mr. and Mrs. Harmon and Carl worked like a charm. As I described class activities, Carl completed my sentences with enthusiasm and added his own comments—in sign, of course. His parents were amazed at his sudden change. Soon Carl was teaching his classmates more signs, and, as the days passed, I saw the children using those signs. By the school year's end, Carl's parents reported that he was signing with them at home and in public. My memories of Mrs. Scott's kids stirred.

In 1984, the Dolton Parent Teacher Association nominated me for the National PTA Outstanding Educator award. I didn't win, but here are some comments the mothers and teachers wrote on the nomination form.

"Ruth Reppert's most accomplished goal would probably be her commitment to education and her sensitivity to communication which may stem from being raised by deaf parents. Perhaps her most gratifying achievement is her mastery of American Sign Language which she teaches to her students...Mrs. Reppert also displays a unique ability of identifying special need children early, so that referrals can be completed and support services assigned...A basic respect for the individual--student, parent, coworker--is reflected in this teacher's approach to all that she does...Perhaps one of her greatest strengths is her patent ability to assert herself... I've never seen her use this formidable skill for anything but improvement."

I felt honored by the nomination, and I treasured the letters from my student teachers, mothers, and students, for they touched my heart. Their comments assured me that my Deaf self was alive and well, and my teaching did not fall on deaf ears...

Ruth in the Lincoln School Classroom

From the day we married, life flowed smoothly for us and for my folks until an unexpected event in the spring of 1973 changed things.

One afternoon Dad told us, *"This morning I was walking on 119th Street to our savings and loan bank to take care of business when someone shoved me from behind, and I stumbled forward. When I turned around, I saw two men scowling at me, and their lips were moving. One of them held out an upturned palm, so I knew he wanted money."*

Anxiously, I questioned, *"What did you do?"*

Dad acted it out. He pointed to his ears while shaking his head no, said, "I am Deaf" in his worst speech, and pulled his trousers' empty side pockets inside out. Then he raised his eyebrows, shrugged his shoulders, and held his palms up.

"What happened next?" I asked with bated breath.

Dad chuckled. *"The men looked at me, looked at each other, shrugged THEIR shoulders, and walked away. I turned around and came back home."*

We were relieved, and I said, *"Dad practices what he preaches. He thinks!"*

But Dad wasn't finished with his story. He reached into a back pocket and withdrew a wad of cash. Waving it proudly, he announced, "They forgot about my back pockets," and he laughed in triumph.

Bob and I gave each other a knowing look. News was appearing in the newspaper about increasing crime in their neighborhood, and Dad's experience emphasized a stark reality: their deafness made Mother and Dad easy victims. This recent happening showed that it was unsafe for them to live in that area any longer. We begged them to look for a new house, preferably in our community, but, even though they agreed with our reasoning, they made no effort to explore the real estate market. We had no clue of what they already had in mind.

When Mother turned sixty-five in December, she and Dad announced they were retiring and moving to Florida! I was shaken. How could I watch out for them at that distance? Their willingness to leave me shattered my illusion that they depended on me. I felt hurt and abandoned. Nevertheless, I stayed calm to listen to their reasoning.

"A Deaf realtor is selling condominium apartments in Margate, a suburb of Fort Lauderdale in Broward County," Mother said, "and all the condos are in the same building. It's called, 'Apple Green.' Many of our friends are buying those condos and retiring there." And Dad said, *"We like the idea. For a long time, we have felt isolated by the big city distances separating us from our friends. Now, we all can be close."* They were excited, and they beamed at us in agreement.

Bob and I smiled and wished them well, but my mind was busy, trying to picture what this move would mean to them and to us. A sudden sadness overcame me, and I felt a lump in my throat. Dad's adage came to mind: "Cheer up, the worst is yet to

153

come," and I tried to convince myself that this was a relatively minor event. I refused to cry.

As I thought about it, I understood why members of the Deaf culture prefer to live close to each other and why they have clubs for socializing. In the Deaf World, sign language makes communicating easy. At Apple Green, my folks and their friends would feel very much at home.

With resignation, Bob and I helped my parents pack their belongings. I will never forget my sadness as we stood on their porch and watched the moving van pull away. Life would never be the same...

One memorable summer evening in 1976, the phone rang, and Bob took the call. "It's for you," he said, so I came to answer it. I said, "Hello?" and was greeted by a man's voice.

"Is this Ruth Reppert?"

"Yes, it is."

"Is your father Edwin M. Hazel?"

"Yes, he is."

"I'm calling from the Margate Hospital. Your father and mother have just been admitted by way of the Emergency Room. They were hit by a car."

"They?" "Father AND mother?" "Hit by a car?" It took a while for the words to sink in, and they didn't make sense. How could this have happened?

154

Dazed and in panic mode, I jotted down the hospital's address, thanked him, and hung up. Bob made our plane reservations, and I made a TDD call to a Deaf neighbor of my folks in Apple Green, asking him to meet us at the Fort Lauderdale airport the next day and drive us to the condo to pick up Dad's car. (I had copies of all the keys.) He kindly agreed to meet us.

Bob and I were at the airport plenty early the next morning only to find that our flight was canceled! How could we inform that Deaf neighbor of our delayed arrival?

Public places recently were required to have a TDD available for their patrons, so we asked at the information desk about the location of a TDD. "A what?" asked the man, and I explained it was a telephone device for the Deaf, a little keyboard that sent typed messages through the telephone wires. "Oh," he said, "I think that machine is in the administrative office," and he directed us to the far end of the airport.

We trekked to that distant office and asked the man inside for the TDD. After a search, he found it in a desk drawer, set it on top, dusted it off, plugged it in, and connected it to his phone.

I typed our friend's phone number, but nothing happened; the battery was dead. "I'm sorry," the man said, "it needs charging. I guess nobody has used this TDD for a while." I said nicely, "It's no wonder! How can passengers know a TDD is located here? We saw no sign anywhere in the airport that alerts passengers of a TDD's availability and its location." He looked embarrassed and said, "You're right. I'll pass that information to my supervisor." Bob and I thanked him for his trouble and left. It seemed that, every time Deaf people made progress, it was "two steps forward and one step backward."

We arrived in Fort Lauderdale two hours late, and our friend was patiently waiting. He drove us to Apple Green, and, as planned, we picked up my folks' car and headed straight for the hospital.

At the hospital's front desk, we discovered that Mother and Dad were in different rooms. First, we went to see Dad. His leg was in a cast, and he was sedated. Then, we went to see Mother. Her right arm was isolated and awaiting surgery. She was relieved to see us and told us what happened.

"Dad and I were returning to Apple Green from an evening walk when we reached the corner across from our building on State Road 7. No traffic light is there, and it is a four-lane highway, so we carefully crossed two of the four lanes and stopped in the pedestrian area. We stood there, waiting for traffic to clear so we could safely cross, when, suddenly, an oncoming car knocked me down."

She asked, "Where is Dad?" and I replied, "He's fast asleep in a room down the hall, and his leg is in a cast. I think I will ask if both of you can be placed in the same room." Mother perked up and exclaimed brightly, "Oh! That would be so much better. Then I can tell Dad what the doctors and nurses say, and we can talk to each other, too."

I left Bob with Mother and went to find the hospital director. "How may I help you?" he asked. I told him that my mother and father were patients, and they were unhappy to be in different rooms. I asked, "Would you please put them together in the same room?"

He smiled. "I am SO sorry, ma'am, but that is against hospital policy. I cannot put a male and a female in the same room." I replied pleasantly, "I'm glad you are sorry, sir, for that shows you are open to reason. Please hear me out, for this is a unique situation."

"First of all, this male and female are married. Second, they both are Deaf and communicate by sign language. Third, my father does not speak or read lips, so doctors and staff would need to write back and forth with him. My mother, however, does speak, and she reads lips, so she can help staff communicate with her husband. By putting them together, you enable them to fully participate in their treatment and recovery."

The man looked at me blankly for a moment and then asked, "What are your parents' names? I'll see what I can do." I gave the names to him and thanked him for his consideration. Then I returned to Mother's room and brought her up to date. After our visit, and noting that Dad was still sleeping, Bob and I left the hospital.

But we didn't drive to the condo. We went straight to the local police station and asked to see the police report of the accident. The clerk got it for us, and we read, "An elderly couple used poor judgment and stepped into the path of the oncoming vehicle." I knew this was not the true story. Deaf folks use their sharp eyes to make up for their lack of hearing. I calmly asked to speak to the officer who had filed the report, and a young policeman appeared to tell his story.

"When I arrived at the scene, I had trouble talking with the victims. The man kept pointing to his ear and mouth when I spoke to him, and the woman was in shock, so I questioned the bystanders. They described the car, said it did not stop, and pointed in the direction it traveled."

"I drove for a few miles and spotted the car parked in front of a 7-Eleven store. Going inside, I found a nervous teenager who admitted his car hit your folks and claimed they had foolishly stepped into his lane. I wrote his account on my report."

My sting of injustice was strong, but I felt no anger. I thanked the officer for speaking with us, and Bob asked the clerk for a copy of the accident report. She gave one to him, and, as we drove away, I read the form closely, focusing on a line titled, "Witness." Beside that word were written a name, address, and telephone number. We stopped at a public phone, I hurriedly dialed the number, and a woman answered. It was the witness! Identifying ourselves, I asked if we could meet with her to hear her account of the accident, and she warmly welcomed us to come at any time. We drove straight there.

Estelle Estes, a woman about our age, invited us inside and told us her story. "I'm a nurse," she said, "and I was driving home from work, traveling north on State Road 7, when I saw two adults ahead and to my left, standing in the island waiting area. Their backs were toward me, so they obviously were waiting to finish crossing to the other side."

"Suddenly, a car appeared, traveling south at high speed. Drifting out of its lane into the waiting area, it sideswiped the couple and knocked them onto the highway. Then, it swerved back into its rightful lane and kept driving south."

"I was shocked at the sight and decided to stop to see if I could give first aid. But, by the time I parked my car and got to the scene, a police car had arrived, and an officer was in control. I told him I saw the whole thing, so he asked me to sign his report as witness."

This account made sense! All of a sudden, I felt relieved, exhausted, and hungry, for it had been a long day, so I discreetly signed to Bob, *"Home?"* and he took over, thanking Miss Estes for caring enough to stop at the scene and for giving her name as witness. Bidding her goodbye, we left.

We drove to the condo, unpacked, grabbed a bite to eat, and returned to the hospital in time for evening visitation. When we gave my parents' names at the front desk, the clerk gave us ONE room number!

We hurried to it, and there were Mother and Dad, smiling broadly, overjoyed to be in the same room. On the way out after our visit, I left a note for the director thanking him for his efforts.

Bob flew back to Chicago and returned to work while I stayed in Florida, waiting for their doctors to pronounce my folks ready for physical therapy. The doctors released them after three weeks, and, with Mother's arm in a sling and Dad in a wheelchair, we flew to rejoin Bob.

Mother and Dad stayed with us during weeks of therapy and were able to return to Margate before I resumed teaching in September. They still faced a long period of painful rehabilitation exercises, and their faithful Deaf friends and neighbors volunteered to transport them to those sessions.

Miss Estes said she would gladly testify if we went to court, but that turned out to be unnecessary. Our lawyer contacted the young man's parents, and their insurance company eventually paid all of Mother and Dad's medical bills and gave my parents a small sum for their pain and suffering.

Distance did not change our relationship; I remained my parents' advocate and their interpreter. Those roles came naturally.

The following year, Mother and Dad's lifelong dream came true. They bought a house not far from the Apple Green condo, and, for the downpayment, they used the money eked out and saved over the years and the sum gained from their accident. This house had six large rooms and a Florida room, and the address was 5380 Southwest 6th Place, Margate. There would be plenty of room for family to stay when they visited...

Distance separated us from Mother and Dad, but we held fast to our family ties. We traveled to Florida each Christmas, and they came to stay with us every summer to escape Florida's hottest months. By 1973, when my folks retired there, our basement recreation room had gone through changes. It first was a children's playroom, then a teen hangout, and finally, a three-room apartment with bath, the perfect place for my parents' summer visits.

Each summer I noticed my folks aging a bit more, with the signs far more evident in Dad. Although his jaunty and pleasant spirit remained steady, his walk became shuffled, his memory was increasingly faulty, and he often repeated himself. These indications were painful reminders that my precious Daddy was nearing the end of his life.

My mind refused to think about it, so I concentrated on work, travel, fun, and entertainment, telling myself, "I'll think about it when the time comes." Well, when I least expected it, the time came.

During the summer of 1983, Mother and Dad were enjoying their annual visit with us when Dad suddenly fell ill with a fever, and he was having trouble breathing. Doctors discovered that his lungs were scarred, probably due to a lifetime of working with lead, touching it and breathing it as he worked on the Monotype machines. But this wasn't the main cause of his distress. Tests showed he had pneumonia caused by an organism so rare that there was no medicine known that could conquer it. Dad's fever raged, and he slipped into a coma.

As Mother and I sat at Dad's bedside, watching his life ebb away, memories crowded my mind, and I recalled what he wrote in my autograph book: "I am with you in spirit, in your efforts at home, at school, at work, and at play." So, when Daddy breathed his last on Thursday, November 3, 1983, I mentally added the words "and in death" to the end of that inscription. My beloved father would be with me in spirit forever.

His strong hands were still, yet they once spoke, telling me of his love, his faith and trust in me, his belief in my abilities, his hopeful worldview, and his wise philosophy of life.

His ears could not hear, yet he listened. His eyes were ever ready to learn and understand my concerns, my worries, my fears, and my joys.

His lips bravely struggled to speak my language, and his speech, peculiar to others, was music to my ears. Wise sayings and sage advice came from those lips, now stilled. It hurt to realize I would never hear my father's voice again.

His eyes were closed, but I signed to him, *"Daddy, thank you for loving me and believing in me. I hope my life will be a testimony to your wisdom, to your love, and to your selfless devotion."*

I kissed his forehead and arranged the lone hairs bravely clinging to his bald head, preserving the moment in memory.

Suddenly, I was overcome with an urge to tell the world about the wonder of this man whom I was blessed to have as my father. I sat at my typewriter and wrote a tribute to Dad, immediately mailing it to the Chicago Tribune and hoping a reporter would see my letter and use it to write an article about Dad. When a laudatory banner obituary, written by Kenan Heise, appeared in the November 8 issue of the Chicago Tribune, it somehow eased my sorrow..

Mother returned to Margate and bravely adjusted to being single. She learned to drive at her ripe age, and, not too surprisingly, she managed her household affairs well, served as the secretary of the Club, pursued her social life within the Deaf community, and encouraged and coached sign language interpreters.

All went well for a while, but, in 1984, Mother's doctors discovered she had chronic lymphocytic leukemia and was weakened by the disease. Bob and I tried to convince her to return to Chicago to live with us, but she stubbornly refused, saying, "No, I can't stand the bitter Chicago winters. But don't worry, I'll be all right because I can depend on my friends." And, sure enough, members of the Club rallied around her while she underwent chemotherapy.

One day I said to Bob, "That familiar sense of responsibility for my parents is nagging me. I wish we could move to Margate to help Mother." I was feeling blue, and I only wanted some comforting. I knew my wish was utterly impractical, for Bob was at the peak of his earning career as vice president of his company, and, to qualify for a full pension, I had to teach in Illinois for six more years.

Without hesitation, Bob cheerfully replied, "I'll start packing!" I could hardly believe my ears, and, with tears of joy, I ran to him with a hug. Our house sold quickly, and our neighbors, friends, and coworkers gave us farewell parties. The partings were bittersweet.

In June 1985, with mixed emotions, Bob and I headed south, bidding farewell to the past and focusing on the future. We were tightening family ties.

III
RETURNING
1985-2016

"Teach children how they should live,
and they will remember it all their life."

Proverbs 22:6 GNT

Chapter 7

REAL WORLD

B etween 1985 and 2016, the Hearing World has cell phones, DVDs, iPods, iPhones, iPads, the World Wide Web, and social networking.

In the Deaf World, the Americans with Disabilities Act (ADA) is passed, there are Video Relay Services (VRS), Video Remote Interpreting (VRI) services, and ASL is taught in schools as a "foreign" language.

When we arrived in Margate, we moved into the big house with Mother, and I got a license to substitute teach. Bob retired, was chief cook and chauffeur for Mother, and concentrated on his hobby, woodworking.

After teaching a few times, I told them I definitely did not enjoy being a substitute teacher. "Why don't you become a qualified sign language interpreter?" Mother asked. "All you have to do is pass the Florida Registry of Interpreters for the Deaf (FRID) Quality Assurance Test (QA)." That sounded unrealistic. In fact, it sounded impossible, for I had not interpreted for over thirty years. But Mother urged, "We need more qualified interpreters here." I said I'd think about it. That possibility had never occurred to me.

Meanwhile, we began to go with her to the Saturday night meetings of the Broward County Association of the Deaf (BCAD, the Club). I felt at home in the crowd, and Bob and I enjoyed chatting with members and winter visitors. Soon, Mother had a suggestion.

"Why don't you come with me to the FRID meeting next week? Interpreters who have passed the state QA Test are interviewing a few Deaf adults in order to demonstrate voicing to sign language students. It should be interesting."

I considered it and said, "All right, I'll go with you on one condition: you must not call any attention to me. I want to become familiar with the local scene without being noticed." She agreed to honor my request.

We arrived after the meeting started and slipped into back row seats. In front, several Deaf adults sat on a platform facing an audience of about fifty people, and I recognized the host, a Hearing visitor to whom Mother had introduced me at the Club. He presented Mr. Davis, a Deaf gentleman sitting on the platform. When an interpreter signed a question to Mr. Davis, he began to answer in ASL. The interpreter hesitated and then stopped; she was having difficulty reading his signing. "I need help!" she cried out as Mr. Davis continued signing his response, unaware of the problem. No one offered aid.

Without warning, the host called to me: "Ruth! Can you help us out here?" Startled, I jumped to my feet and voiced for the gentleman as he continued his story. He ended with a joke, and, after everyone laughed, he sat down, and so did I. The next Deaf participant was introduced, and the program continued smoothly.

Instead of being unnoticed, I was now very much in view. After the meeting ended, a number of interpreters came to comment on my voicing and to thank me for the quick rescue. I was totally surprised that I was not as rusty as I thought and soon decided to consider this path.

I began to attend FRID meetings where state qualified interpreters generously shared their knowledge and experience with newcomers. I learned about the RID Code of Ethics based on respect for Deaf clients and on their right to privacy, and I absorbed all the information and advice I could find. In addition, I read books picturing signs used in specialized fields, such as medical and legal signs, striving to enlarge my sign vocabulary. I kept on studying and learning until I felt ready for the FRID QA test.

I was nervous when I took that test, but I passed at the highest level. My certificate is dated April 5, 1986. The members of the Club congratulated me, and, when I thanked them, they teased, *"You are 'Half-Hearing and Half-Deaf.'"* They didn't know that they described exactly the way I feel!

Soon I was hired as the full-time staff interpreter at a Deaf service agency in a neighboring suburb. It was hard to believe that I hopped back into the Deaf World after an absence of over a quarter of a century. I had traveled full circle...

Bob and I visited the Club regularly, and we became acquainted with most of the members. One man caught my eye, and I asked about him. I learned that His name was Paul, and he was Deaf AND blind. Never having met such a person, I was curious, so I watched him as he chatted with friends nearby. I studied them for a while and then decided to try to communicate with Paul using the same method.

Walking to him, I tapped his shoulder, and he cupped his hand to receive my fingerspelling. After I spelled my name into his palm, he smiled broadly and exclaimed with clear speech, "Oh, you are the Hazels' daughter, I know about you. Please find my wife, Thelma, and introduce yourself. Do you think you can visit us next week? I think you will enjoy seeing my special equipment."

I lightly placed his hands on my wrists and signed *"Thank you, I would like to come. I will ask Thelma to tell me the best day for my visit."* Then I left to find Thelma. She graciously invited me to their condo, gave me the address, and we set a date.

When I pressed the button outside their apartment, I saw the doorbell lights flashing to announce my arrival, and I fully expected Thelma to answer the door. But, when it opened, there stood Paul!

"Hello, Ruth, I surprised you, didn't I? See this wristwatch? It vibrates when the doorbell rings, and it has numbers in braille so I can feel the time. Thelma wears a watch like this one, too. We use our watches to summon each other."

Chuckling, he beckoned me to follow him inside, and, waving to Thelma in the kitchen, I trailed Paul into a small room equipped with two chairs and some machines. We settled in the chairs, and Paul proudly began his demonstration. "Watch how I phone my Deaf friend and have a chat with him," he said. I could see that his phone was connected to a regular TDD, but wait! This TDD had a braille keyboard, and attached to it was a little device that held a roll of paper. Interesting!

Paul turned on the TDD, typed a phone number, and we waited. "Now watch what happens when my friend answers my call," he said. A few seconds passed, and I heard ticking sounds as the little device produced a series of tiny bumps on its paper and then stopped. "These markings mean 'Go Ahead' in braille," Paul explained, "that's TDD terminology."

He then typed a short message on his TDD and sent it out. As the friend's answer came ticking in, Paul ran the tips of his fingers across the dot patterns, line by line, decoding his friend's typed response. When their brief conversation ended, Paul hung up.

I took his incredible hands, put them on my wrists, and signed my amazement at his equipment that enabled him to recognize the doorbell, feel the time, summon his wife, and have telephone conversations with his Deaf friends. Then I asked him the history of his disabilities.

"It is a genetic mutation, *U-s-h-e-r S-y-n-d-r-o-m-e.* I was born deaf, slowly lost my vision, and was completely blind by the time I was twenty-five. Nevertheless, I've learned to get along fine. In fact, reading is my hobby! See this pile of books? They are all printed in braille. I borrow books from the library every two weeks."

I was awestruck by Paul's resilience. The joy he expressed in his daily life touched me, and I was impressed by his unconquerable spirit. I left wishing that the inventors of those devices could see how their amazing inventions enrich lives...

I felt right at home when I interpreted in school settings. Sometimes, though, it was a frustrating experience, for the RID Code of Ethics forbade an interpreter to step out of the interpreting role while on the job. I especially remember Ronnie, a spunky little Deaf boy in fourth grade to whom I was assigned for the entire school day.

I filed into a physical education class along with Ronnie and his classmates, and we took our seats. I interpreted for him while the teacher, Miss Lily, explained the day's activity.

"We will square dance while we listen to a recording. As the dance music plays, you will hear a man's voice telling you what to do and how to step in time to the music. Listen, and be quick to do what he tells you."

Miss Lily arranged the students to stand in a circle and then she started the compact disc. The Hearing children responded almost instantly to the dance calls, but Ronnie was always a few seconds behind the others. He was delayed because it took a few seconds for me to mentally process the call, to sign it, and for Ronnie to then perform the steps. Ronnie did everything correctly, and, although he was a bit behind the other students, he did not hinder them, but happily joined in the square dance, smiling, clapping, and enjoying himself.

When class was over, the children lined up at the classroom door to leave. I stood beside my little client, advancing with him as he moved forward in the line toward Miss Lily who stood at the door. As the children were leaving the classroom, she stuck a gold star on each forehead. When she placed a star, she smiled and exclaimed brightly, "Good job!"

At Ronnie's turn, he looked up at the teacher in happy anticipation, but she scowled and shook her head no. I was surprised and disheartened but kept calm as I interpreted her words and manner. "You don't get a star, Ronnie, you were too slow."

An astonished Ronnie looked questioningly at me and then, unexpectedly and in a flash, he bent down and picked up a gold star that had been lying unnoticed on the floor at Miss Lily's feet where she must have dropped it.

To the teacher's astonishment and to mine, Ronnie promptly licked the star, stuck it on his forehead, and gleefully skipped out of the room. As I followed him out the door and passed Miss Lily, I marveled at her insensitivity, and I was very thankful that she apparently had not injured this resourceful little boy's spirit.

I wonder about the placement of Deaf children in classrooms with Hearing teachers who have no understanding of deafness and with Hearing classmates who cannot communicate directly with them. I'm sure Dad would not have liked it at all...

In the fall of 1986, at the urging of my Deaf friends at the Club, I applied to take the national RID test. At the time, there were very few local sign language interpreters authorized to work in legal settings. If I passed the test and earned national sanction, I would be accredited to interpret in court.

I took the test which began with an interview by a small group of evaluators. As I recall, one was Deaf and several were Hearing, and I didn't know any of them. I was then required to watch videos to sign for Hearing speakers and to voice for Deaf signers. The test was demanding, and I did my best.

In July the long-awaited envelope from the RID arrived in the mail. When I withdrew the contents and read the results, I was shocked! My scores were so low that, without question, I failed the test. There would be no RID status for me.

When I got over my disappointment, I showed my scores to Mother, and she was angry. "Someone has made a mistake," she insisted. "You must question these scores, they can't be yours." "No," I replied, "I will accept the facts: I do not meet the national RID standards. I will be content to interpret in the limited situations allowed for a state QA interpreter, and I will not be able to interpret in court." Mother dropped her argument, and I dropped the subject. For me, it was a painful reality.

The following day, one of my coworkers at the agency asked me, "Have you heard from the RID?" "Yes," I said, "and I failed the test." With that, she complained loudly. "I found out yesterday that one of your evaluators works for our rival agency. Since she is one of the few RID interpreters in town, it would be in that agency's interest for you to fail. She should not have been one of your evaluators because she had a conflict of interest!" I found my friend's view of events hard to believe, so I said, "Whatever the case, I definitely do not plan to challenge my scores."

I didn't go to the next meeting at the Club. I wasn't ready to face the many Deaf clients for whom I had been interpreting and who showed great confidence in me. I was embarrassed by my failure. Bob drove Mother to the meeting and came back home. When he picked her up later, she returned with this report.

"I announced to the crowd that you failed the RID test, and you should have seen the uproar. No one could believe that you failed, and many kept signing *'Impossible!'* One of the members immediately wrote a petition testifying to the high quality of your interpreting and asking the RID to grant you a retest."

"Oh, NO!" I said, "Please stop them. I don't want to take the test again." Mother said, "I can't stop them, the petition is already circulating."

When I discussed the matter with Bob, I was in conflict. "I don't want to cause any trouble, yet I don't want to reject their well-intended efforts."

"Why not give it another try?" he said. "Do it for the Deaf people who need interpreters in court."

"But I might fail again!"

"That's always a possibility."

That thought unnerved me, and I struggled with fear for a long time. Finally, I decided to take the risk, and I appealed to the RID for a retest on the basis of an evaluator having a conflict of interest. I enclosed the BCAD petition in my letter; every member of the Club had signed it.

The RID granted my request on condition that I take a different version of the test in a nearby state. This would eliminate any politics from affecting the results. So Bob and I drove to that state, I took the new test, and the envelope from the RID arrived in a few weeks. My hands trembled as I held it, and fear began to stir. If I failed again, how could I ever face all the people who believed in me?

I asked Bob to open the envelope and look at the results so he could gently prepare me if I failed again. He laughed and said, "I think you did well." When he read my scores, he smiled and gave me a hug. "Congratulations," he said, and I sighed with relief. I passed with high scores and earned the RID Comprehensive Skills Certificate (CSC), qualifying me to interpret in all situations. My certificate is dated August 17, 1987. I went to the Club that Saturday, announced the good news, and thanked everyone for their support. By the time I left for home, I had enjoyed many hearty pats on my back. My

Deaf family pulled me through the experience with glowing results.

After spending so many years in a self-contained classroom, I learned a hard lesson about politics in the real world...

Not long afterward, we received an interpreting request, well in advance, from Mr. Philip Bravin, an IBM executive from New York, for an all-day conference on the grounds of the International Business Machines Corporation (IBM) in Boca Raton. As I recall, IBM was going to introduce the PC convertible weighing just thirteen pounds, and speakers would be from the United States and from countries around the world.

I had never owned a computer, so my first reaction was to decline the job. But, setting my hesitation aside, I planned my course. I had to quickly learn the vocabulary and the sign representations, so I bought a book on the subject. Terms like "gigabyte," "kilobyte," "icon," "megabyte," "digitize," "monitor," and "cursor," were like a foreign language to me, but I worked hard to memorize the terms and signs. This would be an historic occasion, and I felt honored to take part in the proceedings.

The day arrived, and I reported to the designated building on the IBM campus. My client was awaiting me at the door, and he led me into a huge auditorium where about twenty men dressed in business suits sat in rows on the stage, facing the audience.

Mr. Bravin was friendly and pleasant as he ushered me to a chair in the aisle facing his end row seat. My back would be to the stage as I signed to him. I was nervous, but I acted my role: calm, cool, and collected. This would be a growing experience.

The first speaker was from Asia, and, when he began to speak English with a thick accent, I knew I was in trouble. I strained to hear syllables, to recognize mispronounced English words, to make sense of each faulty sentence, and to mentally convert it all to ASL for my client. When this speaker sat down, I breathed a sigh of relief, only to find that a great many of the presenters had foreign accents, so my task was stressful all morning. My experience with Dad's speech distortions came to my rescue.

The assembly paused for a break, but I was to have no rest. One of the native English speakers came down to the main floor and was immediately surrounded by a horde of questioning attendees. My client joined them, and I followed into a jam-packed crowd. It was impossible for me to move, much less interpret.

Determined that my client would not be left out, I left Mr. Bravin's side and repeated, "Excuse me," as I politely worked my way through the crowd and stood beside the speaker. From there, I interpreted the questions posed and the answers given. Mr. Bravin showed delight, and I was satisfied.

During the afternoon session, one of the speakers used the word, "motherboard," and, as I signed the term, my facial expression must have betrayed my amusement, for Mr. Bravin, obviously noticing my reaction, smiled as he signed back to me, *"Yes, there really IS a 'motherboard!'"*

At the end of the day, I was mentally and physically exhausted, but I had an exciting idea: now that I know computer terms, maybe I will buy myself a computer....

It was Monday morning, May 23, 1988, shortly after nine, a date ever in my memory. I was sitting at my desk at the agency going over the day's scheduled assignments when I heard the office door open. I was surprised to see Bob! I glanced at my watch. He was supposed to be driving Mother to a nine-thirty appointment. Why was he here?

When he arrived at my desk, he said softly, "Your mother is gone." Puzzled, I asked, "Where did she go?" He repeated his announcement gently, this time with meaningful tone and emphasis on the word "gone." It took a few seconds for me to understand his intended meaning.

I jumped up in panic. "You must be mistaken," I said, "hurry, take me to her." I would come to Mother's aid as I did many times in the past. Bob took my arm, and we hurried out the door. Every fiber of my being was pressing me forward."Hurry! Hurry! Mother needs me," I urged. As Bob drove, he told me what had happened, and his voice echoed in my ears as if he were miles away.

"I wakened early and got ready to drive your mom to her appointment. She didn't come to breakfast, so I went to her bedroom and found her in bed. I thought she was still sleeping, so I tapped her. When she didn't respond, I knew she had passed away."

I rushed into the house. Yes, Mother was in bed, and she did look like she was sleeping, but her flesh was gray. Reality overcame me, and my body, poised to rescue her, went limp. Bob steadied me. No, I could not change this event for Mother, this time I was powerless. The realization was crushing.

I stroked her beautiful hands. They taught signing to me and moved with so much grace that her Deaf friends often begged her to sign poetry for them. With strength, resolve, and self-sacrifice, her hands had labored tirelessly for Dad and me, and for many other folks.

Her ears were hushed long ago, but her inner ear rang with the songs of her childhood, and I often overheard her singing in her sweet monotone voice.

Her keen eyes missed nothing. They discerned the feelings and intents of others by their faces, their eyes, and their body language, and they skillfully read lips with little effort.

Her own lips spoke English so clearly that Hearing folks often didn't realize she was Deaf. Those lips modeled speech for me, and they spoke of practical matters, ever ready to answer my questions.

I recalled the poem by Grillet that she wrote in my sixth grade autograph book. "I shall pass through this world but once; any good thing that I can do, or any kindness I can show to any fellow-creature, let me do it now; let me not defer nor neglect it, for

I shall not pass this way again." Now I understood! Mother lived this kind of life.

I signed to her for the last time. *"Thank you, my dear Mother, for your tender heart, strengthened by much adversity and devoted to others. May my life reflect your strength, your courage, and your faithfulness."* I softly kissed her goodbye. Though gone from my presence, she would forever be in my heart.

I immediately prepared a memorial service to be held at our church where Deaf and Hearing guests soon joined us in a tribute. Son-in-law, Bob, welcomed Deaf guests in sign, grandson, Jim, delivered the message, granddaughter, Linda, interpreted the speaking, and I interpreted a hymn. Mother would have been pleased, for she was fiercely proud of her signing family.

The best compliment I've received was given me by my Deaf friends: "You sign like your mother."...

I took time off after Mother's death, but I was soon back to work. Keeping busy would be healing. Assignments from IBM were awaiting me, and I found myself there regularly, interpreting for several Deaf employees. One was Gary Behm, an Advanced Process Control project manager. He spoke well for himself, so my job usually consisted of signing what others on his team said during their department meetings. During our lunch breaks, I learned that Gary knew Tom and Julia and our other Deaf friends, so Bob and I were soon socializing with Gary and his Deaf wife, Jeanne, often visiting them in their home.

We grew fond of their little Hearing son, Byron, and I liked to observe his interactions with his parents, for it reminded me of how I signed at an early age. Although Gary and Jeanne spoke English well, they signed ASL with each other and with Byron, too. He was a smart little fellow, and, not surprisingly, I often noticed indications that he sensed some responsibility for his parents.

When a second child was due, I agreed to interpret at the baby's birth. Jeanne explained, "The doctor will wear a mask, and I won't be able to lipread his directions." When I got the call, I hurried to the hospital, scrubbed up, donned a green outfit, and reported to the birthing room. This was a "first" in my interpreting career, and it was thrilling!

This second son, Cory, was found to be deaf, and, when a third son, Derrick, was born deaf, Byron was now the only Hearing member in a family of five for whom he surely felt somewhat responsible at times. In some ways, I was observing a replay of my own childhood, and my compassion and empathy for Byron were strong.

Bob and I sometimes babysat with the boys. I entertained them with kindergarten songs, games, and stories, while Bob did card tricks and showed Byron how to play chess. It fascinated us to watch the boys sign in ASL so fluently. Occasionally, I pointed out to Byron how our lives were somewhat similar.

I wasn't surprised to learn that, when Byron reached adulthood, he became a sign language interpreter and a teacher of Deaf high school students. I wonder if he feels "Half-Hearing and Half-Deaf" as I do. In fact, I wonder if many, if not all, CODAs feel that same way...

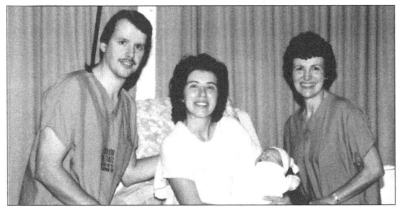

The Behms
Gary, Jeanne, Cory, and Ruth
December 30, 1988

Dad's message was fixed in my mind: *"I hope, when you grow up, you will teach Hearing people about the Deaf and Deaf culture and show them how to sign with us."* So I started an evening class in Contact Signing, signing in English sentences. This was the mode Mother and many of her friends used, and what I first learned. That learning was quick and easy, but learning to sign with Dad and to understand ASL took much longer.

I chose "Sign Language Made Simple," a book written by a professor, Edgar D. Lawrence. It follows the same approach of textbooks I used, and, with one class a week, it teaches fifteen hundred ASL signs in less than a year, perfect for basic everyday conversations.

Twenty-four people enrolled in my first class ranging in age from eight to sixty and coming from all walks of life—scuba diver, housewife, nurse, social worker, etc. Interest was high, and the students were enthusiastic.

One evening a student teasingly said, "Ruth, I wish we could take you home with us to help us practice the movements." That remark gave me an idea! I contacted the book's author and asked if he was interested in having a demonstration video to go with his book, and he was! So, in 1990, Bob and I produced the "Practice Videotape for Sign Language Made Simple" in which I demonstrate all of the signs and sentences. My students made rapid progress with me coaching them at home on video, now on DVD.

There were many classes in which I not only taught signing but also talked about deafness, Deaf culture, and Deaf history, and I regularly invited Deaf friends to be interviewed. At the end of each series of classes, I always asked my students for feedback. Here is a favorite evaluation.

"With this textbook and Practice Video, learning to sign has been easy and fun. I like reviewing and practicing my lessons at home with the video. I have had occasion to use my new skills and to help my bank customers quickly and efficiently. I heartily recommend that you learn to sign with 'Sign Language Made Simple' materials. You, your employer, and the next Deaf person you meet will be glad you did. (signed) Kimberly, Margate, FL."

I could almost hear Dad say, "Thank you, Ruth Ann..."

Sign Language Class
Flashing the "I Love You" sign (ILY)
Ruth is standing on the right.

Interpreting was a role thrust upon me early in life, and I dutifully performed it to please Mother and Dad. However, I was now a professional interpreter in a new era, and each assignment was a novel adventure. I often told Bob, "I am getting an education unlike anything one gets inside a classroom." My new career was challenging, with some events that stand out in my memory. Here are my favorites.

I especially remember the time I joined a team of interpreters accompanying a group of Deaf people on a Caribbean cruise. At our request, the captain accommodated the Deaf passengers by allowing them to enter the theater early to occupy the front row seats facing the right side of the stage. This provided the best view of the evening performances and the interpreters, as well.

185

I was not on duty the first night, so I sat behind the front rows of Deaf clients, waiting for the show to begin. Suddenly, I heard a loud voice somewhere behind me. "These people have their nerve. They come early and grab front seats." Another voice remarked, "Yeah, one on one, they seem nice enough, but when they get together, they're pushy." I turned to identify the speakers, but, just then, the lights dimmed, the curtain rose, and I lost a teaching opportunity.

When the Deaf passengers entered the theater on the second night, their front seats were already taken by Hearing folks! So, on the third night, the cruise director cordoned off that section well in advance of the show and posted a "reserved" sign. The faces of the Hearing passengers, arriving early to claim a front seat, reflected their utter disgust.

It was unnerving to witness firsthand how stereotypes can be based on misunderstanding. Regretfully, in this situation, misunderstanding prevailed...

I decided to attend a meeting that promised to be productive. As I recall, its purpose was to foster communication between sign language interpreters and their clients. I was sitting in a front section of an auditorium with a group of my fellow interpreters, a closely-knit and cooperative group. In the remaining seats were members of the local Deaf community, many of whom were our clients at one time or another.

One of the Deaf attendees mounted the stage and scolded us. *"You interpreters do not always voice correctly for us. I know, because I read your lips. It is awful, and it is embarrassing, too. You need to watch us more closely."* Another stood up and made a similar criticism. Dissatisfaction was in the air.

Regrettably, their complaint was based on reality, so we interpreters sat quietly. Not one of us moved to respond amidst the awkward pause. Then, for some reason that I don't yet understand, I mounted the stage, and, planting one "frog foot" in each culture, I addressed my dear Deaf family on behalf of their Hearing interpreters. Perhaps I was presumptuous, but I had no time to ponder. I appealed to one of the interpreters, asking her to voice for me.

"Thank you, friends, for your honest feedback. We interpreters strive to do our best. It is true, there might be occasions when we cannot voice correctly for you, and there is good reason for this. If you sign and fingerspell too fast, then our eyes can't grasp what you are saying, and we are stuck. I will demonstrate."

I acted out a worst case scenario; I fingerspelled and signed so fast that no one could possibly know what I said. Then, I slowed my signing. *"If it is impossible for us to ask you to repeat, we must do the best we can. It frustrates us."* I heard sounds of surprise and understanding coming from our clients as I went on with my explanation.

"If you will sign and fingerspell slowly and clearly, the interpreter can understand you and will voice properly. You and your interpreter will become a successful team. How many of you are willing to cooperate with your interpreter in this way?"

All the Deaf attendees enthusiastically raised their hands in reply. "*Wonderful!*" I said, and the entire audience joined me in hand-waving applause.

When I returned to my seat, I felt my elation quickly change to embarrassment. My thoughts were reeling. What possessed me to speak up? Did I make a fool of myself? What did my Hearing associates think of this? Did they resent my speaking on their behalf? Would I be the object of their derision? I sank back into my seat trying to sort my feelings as the meeting moved on to other topics. I consoled myself with the fact that my actions appeared to have improved understanding. If so, my discomfort was worth the result...

Then there was the time I interpreted at city hall. A meeting was requested by several Deaf residents who sought a new provision for the city's Deaf and hard of hearing citizens. City officials sat on a raised platform, and I took my place on the main floor, seated with my back toward them and facing my Deaf clients. Before the meeting began, three of them came to speak to me, one after the other.

The first spoke: "I sign a little, but I depend on my lipreading to understand. Please speak clearly." I answered, pronouncing plainly: "I will try my best."

The second spoke and signed: "*I do not understand ASL. I sign in English sentences, so please keep that in mind when you interpret.*" I spoke and signed, "*I will try my best.*"

The third signed, "I use ASL only, so please sign in ASL." I answered in ASL, "*I will try my best.*"

I knew how these clients felt; none wanted to be left out. How could I satisfy all three? I could try COMBINING the three modes! It might work.

The meeting began, and I proceeded with my plan. I interpreted the speaking by using ASL signs in English sentences, speaking clearly, and quickly inserting the ASL concepts, facial expressions, and gestures, all at the same time. I also voiced for the clients who signed their own comments.

When the meeting ended, those same clients came to bid me goodbye, and, amazingly, each smiled and said, "Thank you, I understood everything!"

This little frog tried to hop, skip, and jump at the same time and apparently succeeded. I had left no one out! Mother and Dad would be pleased...

Even though I studied a book on legal signs and felt well-prepared, every time I entered the courthouse and went through the security station, the feeling of responsibility weighed heavily on my shoulders. The hushed hallways where solemn people milled outside the various courtrooms conveyed the seriousness of the business going on there. One misinterpretation on my part could have damaging effects, so I was on sharp alert. These were the halls of justice, and I was filled with awe and great respect.

Shortly after the ADA took effect, I was standing before a judge, my back to him, and facing a Deaf man who was brought from the jail. I interpreted as the judge spoke to him, explaining the charges and the decision to send the man back to prison. Then he asked, "Do you have anything to say?" The prisoner nodded yes, and I voiced his remarks.

"Your honor, I have been sitting in the jail for over a month, and I haven't been able to enjoy TV programs like the Hearing inmates do. The TV at the jail should have closed captioning."

The judge's voice revealed his disgust as he sarcastically said, "Toooo bad! If you would keep out of trouble and out of our jail, this would not be a problem. Even better, why don't you limit your lawbreaking to another county next time? Maybe they will have closed captioning in their jail." My face reflected the judge's ridicule and sarcasm. When the courtroom laughter faded, he said, "By the way, YOU must pay for your interpreter today," and he gruffly dismissed the prisoner to jail. My job ended.

I stood amazed at this judge's unfamiliarity with the federal law as it applies to Deaf people. In these halls of justice, he had denied justice to my client. I was familiar with the sting this prisoner was feeling. How many more Deaf people would be denied rights by this uninformed judge? Perhaps none if I acted now.

Walking away from the bench, I reached into my purse for a sealed business envelope. Enclosed was our agency's form letter that I prepared for such occasions. It summarized ADA requirements: Deaf persons must receive equal access to communication. Therefore, the court must hire and pay for qualified sign language interpreters. And, whenever possible, Deaf individuals should have other services, including closed captioning on television programs.

Hastily writing the judge's name on the envelope, I stopped at the desk of the Clerk of Court, smiled, and politely asked, "Would you please give this to the judge?" She nodded that she would, and I made my exit. It was all I could do.

The next day, I was surprised to come upon a report of the event in the morning newspaper. The journalist correctly stated the Deaf prisoner's request and the judge's response, but, to my dismay, the writer ridiculed the Deaf man. I imagined readers sipping their morning coffee while reading this column and having their daily laugh. That familiar sting of injustice stirred. It was taking a long time for folks to fully understand the ADA. Just as Dad forewarned, the wheels of justice turn slowly...

I kept a demanding schedule, so Bob insisted we take vacations, many of which were last minute cruises out of nearby Port Everglades. We vacationed with Hearing friends, George and Lois Smith, Chuck and Gean Krueger, Les and Colette Stermer, and Don and Marion Munro. We also traveled with close Deaf friends, for my Deaf self seemed to yearn for their company.

In 1988, we cruised the Caribbean with Tom and Julia and with Frank and Lorraine Sullivan. And, in 1991, Bob and I accompanied Tom and Julia, Don and Agnes Padden, and Jeanne and Justin Lambert to Lake Powell, Utah for a houseboat vacation. Bob was elected the captain, and he skillfully guided us from one awesome sight to another, following the marked channels. The sights were absolutely breathtaking, the company enjoyable.

One day, as he piloted, we were sitting around the table chatting while Julia stood at the stove, her back to us, preparing a huge pot of chili for our lunch.

Suddenly, Bob called out to me, "Ruth! A huge tour boat is heading this way, and its path is way too close to us. Tell Julia to sit down immediately, the waves will soon be rocking the houseboat."

I jumped up, but, before I could reach Julia and tap her, a huge wave slapped the houseboat, and she was thrown off balance. The pot flipped over, crashing to the floor and spattering its contents everywhere.

After a few minutes of rocking and swaying, the houseboat settled, and we watched in amazement at what happened next.

Julia quickly regained her composure, and, not wasting a moment, she scraped all of the chili back into the pot and returned it to the stove. That day we all enjoyed a delicious chili lunch, and we all lived to tell the tale.

I cherished the comradeship, and it didn't occur to me until recently that an added bonus for our Deaf friends was the fact that they had their interpreter along with them on their vacations.

Well, MY bonus was enjoying their company every minute because interpreting for friends and family always gives me much pleasure...

Frank Sullivan and Ruth

Houseboat Vacation

Bob, Tom, Jeanne, Justin, Agnes, Julia, Ruth

Aunt Toni was still a vital part of my life. Although she worked full time, she spent her summer vacations with us, keeping close with me and bonding with Bob and our kids. By 1990 she was the last remaining member of her immediate family, retired after thirty years with her company and living alone in her little house. That summer was a turning point.

Bob and I drove to Texas to visit son Jim in his new apartment, and, when we arrived, he told us that my cousin, Patty, was trying to reach us. She wanted me to know that Toni was in the University of Pittsburgh Medical Center after having surgery. Alarmed, I looked at Bob and said, "I must go to her." He, too, was concerned, so he encouraged me to fly to Pittsburgh the next day, assuring me he would be fine driving home to Florida alone after visiting with Jim.

Patty met my plane and drove us to the hospital. While she parked her car, I hurried to Toni's room and bumped into a man just coming out. He spoke to me.

"Are you a family member?"

"Yes, I am Miss Schifino's niece."

"I'm Dr. Bryant, her surgeon. Your aunt has an advanced case of colon cancer. I removed as much of the diseased tissue as I could and performed a colostomy, but the situation is terminal; she has less than six months to live. I leave it to you to break that news to her. And, by the way, don't bother with chemotherapy; it won't work in a case like this."

He hurried away, leaving me overwhelmed with the bad news. I stood in the hall, wavering: shall I, or shall I not, tell Toni of the doctor's forecast? It didn't take me long to decide that I wouldn't tell her. I walked into Toni's room, and she burst into tears.

"I have colon cancer, and the doctor put a bag on me."

"Other people get used to it," I said calmly, "and so can you. It's a good thing the doctors discovered the cancer in time because, after a few treatments, you should be fine. I'll stay with you until you adjust to your ostomy, it won't take you long."

Her expression slowly changed, and she wiped her tears away. Now she looked determined to adapt to a new way of living, and she smiled!

I stayed with Toni in her home for about three weeks. Then, having hatched a plan with Bob, I told her we invited her to come and live with us. After long thought, Toni accepted, and we worked our plan. Bob flew to Pittsburgh and set off to drive Toni's car to Florida while we packed, reserving a flight to arrive in Fort Lauderdale in time for Bob to meet us at the airport. Meanwhile, Patty and her husband agreed to handle the sale of the little house.

Toni settled in the spare bedroom of the big Margate house that was now ours, and I took her to see Mother's oncologist. He prescribed weekly intravenous chemical drips, and the treatments were almost as hard on me as they were on her.

When Toni was nauseous and too ill to eat, I fought off guilt feelings for putting her through such misery, and I often questioned myself. Was I doing the right thing? Always, my answer was yes. Bob and I clung to hope during those difficult times.

Amazingly, after one year of treatments, Toni's cancer went into remission, and we joyfully celebrated the outcome, wishing we could relay the good news to Dr. Bryant, but we had lost track of him.

Toni regained her vitality. She attended my sign language classes, joined us on cruises, went with us on vacations, and accompanied us on trips to see our kids. We three were having a great time reviving our "sister" relationship.

How sweet it was to have Toni with me on shopping sprees again. She routinely accompanied me to fitting rooms, helped me try on outfits, and gave me her opinion. We didn't always agree, however. Toni was ultra-modern, dressing in the latest colorful styles and wearing trendy glasses. On the other hand, I'm conservative and prefer loose-fitting styles, muted colors, modest necklines, and very little makeup.

When it came to choosing jewelry, Toni claimed, "'Big' is better," but I consider "big" too flashy, so I stubbornly chose "small." Sometimes Toni would tease, "Ruth, when it comes to your tastes, you are older than I am!" I couldn't deny it. Inside of me remains the shy little girl who was so often pushed into view that, as an adult, she dislikes attracting attention to herself in the course of her daily life.

Toni became a beloved member of our family, and we valued each day as a precious gift. Meanwhile, Dr. Bryant's prediction remained a secret...

Ruth Ann and Aunt Toni 1945

Chapter 8

ON A MISSION

Our lives were full and happy, and I was thriving with my new career, but change was in the wind again. One fateful evening in 1991, our telephone rang, and it was Bill, a coworker at our agency. "Hi, Ruth," he said. "I have news. I'm leaving this agency to form a new one, the Deaf Service Center of Broward County (DSC). Would you please consider being the director?"

I caught my breath. This was an opportunity my current agency did not offer. I told him I would think about it and get back to him. After discussing the proposal in depth with Bob, I returned Bill's call and said, "I will consider joining you if you agree to make our new agency focus on educating the public on deafness." Bill surprised me when he said, "No problem! I have that very thing in mind." Bob and I met with him the following evening.

When that meeting was over, Bill was "Director" and I was the "Assistant Director." In this capacity, I would be in the office daily, available to do social work, but I would also be the "Education Program Coordinator." In that role, I would design and carry out educational programs. In both positions, I would be a volunteer, and income to DSC for my services would help fund the agency.

My interpreting services, however, would not be donated. Professional interpreters are paid.

We gave our employer two-week's notice of our departure, and, in 1992, DSC opened its office in Margate, the hub of the local Deaf community. With furniture and equipment donated by Deaf and Hearing supporters, we would soon be launching our new business.

First, however, we met with the leaders of our former agency and explained how DSC's mission was intended to complement theirs. We proposed that our agencies work together to serve the local Deaf community. To our dismay, they declined our proposal, and this meant that the agencies would be in competition, especially for community funding. Disappointed, but undeterred, Bill and I regrouped, formulated our plan, hired an office secretary, and advertised our office hours.

We were a fledgling agency when, on August 28, 1992, Hurricane Andrew was heading toward Ft. Lauderdale. At home that evening, Bob and I were watching TV news announcements regarding the storm when our TDD started flashing. One by one, members of the local Deaf community called us in a panic, wanting to know the status of the storm and the evacuation routes. They had no way to access that information. (TV closed captioning was not yet in effect.) I tried to calm them by telling them I would phone each channel and ask that a sign language interpreter be employed for their station's emergency broadcasts.

I had no idea if I could accomplish this, however. I was just a teacher and a sign language interpreter with a new official position and title. How in the world could I convince the stations to remedy the situation? As I wondered, it came to me: there is power in words!

I used the title of our new agency and of my new position, calling the TV channels one by one and announcing with authority that I was a director of the Deaf Service Center of Broward County and asking to speak to the station manager. Those words got me to the right person each time, and I launched my argument, pointing out that the station was excluding all south Florida Deaf and hard of hearing viewers from lifesaving information. Then I suggested the channel had a moral obligation to provide the emergency information to this population.

The managers listened politely, but all were unmoved—except one. Channel 12 came to the rescue! I gave the phone number of their nearest Deaf service agency to the manager, and, within a short time, a sign language interpreter appeared on that channel, saving the day for the Deaf and hard of hearing community. Fortunately for those in the Fort Lauderdale area, Andrew changed its course that night and struck farther south. The unintended result of winning that interpreting service was an increase in the number of DSC supporters. Our agency was on its way...

On days when I sat in the office with very few clients, I began to visualize possible educational projects. The incidents I recalled from my childhood provided plenty of inspiration, and it was thrilling to now be a director of a county agency with authority to remedy those kinds of situations. It seemed as if a spring inside me, winding tighter and tighter for years, suddenly let loose, driving me into action. My list of projects grew quickly.

Thinking of Mother and Dad's accident, I designed and distributed a wallet-size emergency card. It informed police that the carrier is Deaf and has a civil right to a sign language interpreter. I also contracted with the city of Margate to teach its police and fire fighters how to communicate in their lines of duty with Deaf people.

Because Mother encouraged interpreters, I formed a support group for budding interpreters, "Advancing Interpreters' Mutual Support (AIMS)."

Well aware of the interpreter shortage, I contacted the leaders of Broward Community College and convinced them to start an interpreter training program.

Recalling those frustrating hospital experiences, I designed a course titled "Serving Deaf Patients," and it was adopted by the Florida Board of Nursing as a continuing education option for Florida's nurses.

Because my parents were isolated at their workplaces, I arranged with Broward County government to teach Contact Signing classes to their employees.

Since Dad had difficulty writing English, I held training classes for Broward County 9-1-1 operators on communicating on the TDD with Deaf ASL callers.

I found myself on a mission to help close the gap between the Deaf World and the Hearing World. Broward County Government took notice...

BOARD OF COMMISSIONERS OF BROWARD COUNTY FLORIDA MEETING OF JULY 5, 1994
(The meeting convened at 10 a.m. and adjourned at noon.)
PLEDGE OF ALLEGIANCE -led by Mayor Albert Capellini, city of Deerfield Beach.
THOUGHT OF THE DAY - given by the Chair.
CALL TO ORDER

75. PROCLAMATION - JULY 5, 1994 - "DEAF SERVICE CENTER OF BROWARD COUNTY INC. APPRECIATION DAY" On behalf of the Board, Commissioner Thompson read into the record a proclamation designating July 5, 1994 as "Deaf Service Center of Broward County Inc. Appreciation Day". The Board recognized the Deaf Service Center as a valuable community resource for its foresight and commitment to the county's deaf and hard of hearing populations.

ACTION: (A-158) Ms. Ruth Reppert, Deaf Service Center of Broward County Inc., accepted the proclamation, thanked the Board and introduced the presence of the deaf and hard of hearing individuals at this day's meeting.

Ms. Susan DellCioppia, Personnel Division, acknowledged county staff participating in the county's Sign Language Classes and thanked the Board for initiating this program.

Broward County Minutes

I remember the day I interviewed Dawn at my first agency for the position of Employment Counselor. She told me she was a teacher of Deaf children in New York, newly arrived in town. To better understand what her young students would likely experience in adulthood, she sought work with Deaf adults. I was impressed with her dedication and took an immediate liking to her.

My next task was to observe her signing skills, so I played a recording of a lecture and asked her to interpret it. She was nervous, and her signing needed improvement, but I admired her enthusiasm, her positive attitude, and her willingness to learn. Consequently, I recommended she be hired.

At Dawn's request, we met weekly for "polishing" sessions to work on expanding her signing skills, and she and I became fast friends, even though we are of different generations. I was delighted by her sense of humor and her creativity, and she soon was a frequent and welcome guest in our home. Bob, Toni, and I grew fond of her.

One day I said, "Dawn, if you will allow me, I would like to share all that I have learned about deafness and Deaf people with you." She welcomed my input and was an eager learner. Curious about my life as "the daughter of Ed and Irene," as she put it, she liked to ask questions and get my perspective on a variety of subjects related to deafness and Deaf people. I always prefaced my answers by emphasizing that they were my opinions, and there were other viewpoints she should also consider. It wasn't long before she said, "Thanks for sharing these insights with me, Ruth. I'm beginning to know what it might feel like to be Deaf, and I better understand Deaf people and their culture." Her words gave me heartwarming satisfaction.

Sadly, our close friendship was interrupted when Dawn returned to her first love, the teaching of Deaf children in public school, and Bob, Toni, and I didn't see her quite as often.

But, when DSC opened in 1992, Dawn came to the office and eagerly volunteered her time and talent to the agency. Happy to be reunited, she and I became a productive team of volunteers. There was no end to the ideas that popped into our minds, and we excitedly rushed to carry them out.

Dawn's experience with Deaf children and their parents led to some innovative programs. Among them were: "Kids' Club," where Deaf kids and their Hearing siblings went on monthly field trips; a support group for Hearing parents of Deaf children; and a story hour for Deaf kids at the Broward County Library. And, after we designed and published a monthly newsletter, DSC's membership grew, and its influence expanded.

Dawn and I not only belong to different generations, we differ in religious beliefs: she is Jewish, and I am Christian. We respect each other's views and learn from each other. To improve her interpreting skill, Dawn sometimes attended our church worship service to watch me interpret the sermon. So, when DSC got a request for an interpreter at a Friday night temple service, Dawn encouraged me to accept it as my own learning experience. I did, and Dawn planned to attend and observe.

At the rabbi's suggestion, I met with him on Thursday to get the printed English translation of the Hebrew passages he would read. Then, on Friday night, as he spoke Hebrew, I followed the script, matching my signing to his vocal tone, phrasing, and pauses. After watching, Dawn joked, "The Deaf congregants may have understood the Hebrew passages better than some of the Hearing attendees!"

Before long, Dawn passed the state QA exam and became a professional sign language interpreter. She had worked hard, and her certificate was well-earned.

Dawn and I are friends to this day, bonded by the memory of those exciting days when, together, we were bridging the Deaf and Hearing worlds...

Dawn and Ruth 1990

By this time, Tom and Julia had retired and moved to Margate, reviving our family relationship, and they eagerly accepted an invitation to be on the DSC board of directors. Tom said, "Julia and I still have a lot of ideas and energy." Now, half of DSC's board members were Deaf individuals, an exceptional development.

Historically, such boards consisted of Hearing folks, unfamiliar with deafness, who established programs for the Deaf.

Julia announced her exciting news at a board meeting. "I found a place in Margate for our sign language classes, the Cokesbury United Methodist Church. We can hold evening classes for adults and kids in their Sunday school classrooms." It didn't take us long to begin those classes with Julia, Dawn, and Ruth ready and willing instructors. Soon we were using the church meeting hall for our weekly "Saturday Socials" where a number of Deaf volunteers met and socialized with interpreters and sign language students to promote easy communication.

And Tom applied his experience as a leader in the Deaf community and focused on enlarging our agency's emphasis.

At a planning retreat, he said, "Ruth, DSC's programs that center on communicating with Deaf people are admirable, but I suggest we expand our vision. Let me explain what I have in mind."

"Too long has 'deaf and dumb' been foremost in the public's mind, so I see us sponsoring an annual community program that features successful Deaf people telling their life stories. This will help to overcome stereotypes."

And that is exactly how DSC's annual "Deaf Connection" lectures began. We advertised them to the public, and Tom invited great presenters.

One was Dr. Donalda Kay Ammons, Professor Emerita, Gallaudet University, who taught language, literature, and culture for more than thirty years and was honored by the university for her teaching.

One was popular actress Linda Bove, a star of Sesame Street and a founding member of the National Theater of the Deaf who, in 1974, received the Italian-American Award for her work on television.

Another was Dr. Victor Galloway, Chief of the Deafness and Communications Disorders Branch of the Rehabilitation Services Administration (RSA) for the U.S. Department of Education, more widely known as Meryl Streep's father in the movie, "River Wild."

But Tom didn't stop there. He soon had another idea for enlarging DSC's focus. "Nearby Nova Southeastern University (Nova) can help us educate the Hearing public," he declared with confidence. I was completely astounded, for this was beyond my hopes and dreams. I asked, doubtfully, "How can we get their attention?" He grinned, and I saw that familiar twinkle in his eye. "You'll see," he said.

I soon found myself sitting with Tom in an office at Nova, awaiting an unnamed gentleman's appearance. Tom was explaining that he met with this man earlier and had made a proposal to him when the man arrived. Tom introduced me to Dr. Richard Peterson, the director of continuing education.

"Hello, Ruth, I've heard a lot about you from Tom. I have agreed to support DSC's work by establishing the 'Community Education on Deafness' program here at the university. But, while Nova will sponsor the programs, you are to initiate, organize, and manage them. What do you say to my proposal?"

"I gladly accept it," I replied, "and thank you for sharing our vision."

This happened smoothly due to Tom's groundwork, of course. I was awestruck by his cool expertise. Without his help, I doubted I could gain access to someone in Mr. Peterson's position, let alone win his or her support. Tom made it look so easy!

I soon discovered that Nova's backing gave me greater influence as I set up a class for nurses and recruited more cities to sponsor training for their workers on deafness issues and the ADA. More and more Hearing folks were becoming aware of the Deaf community, and it was exciting to see how those three words, "Nova Southeastern University," made it all possible. Tom recognized the great power in those three words, and so did I.

Tom and Julia were a dynamic duo, expanding DSC's borders and leading us to accomplishments far beyond anything we could have imagined...

In 1996, I was leading a class for Margate's police officers titled, "Serving Deaf Citizens." I reviewed the sections of the ADA referring to the rights of the Deaf and hard of hearing and taught them some signs to use in their work.

At the end of the session, I said, "Here is an example of what you should NOT do," and I began the account of my parents' accident.

A Training Class

"Twenty years ago, my Deaf parents were hit by a car not far from Apple Green on State Road 7. They were standing in an island area, waiting to finish crossing and....." A deputy interrupted, springing to his feet and calling out in excitement.

"I was the officer who reported to that scene! I remember it well. When I tried to talk to the woman, she was in shock and didn't answer, and the man just kept pointing to his ear and mouth. Who would guess that their daughter would be teaching me twenty years later?

For a moment, I was speechless, and the others exclaimed with surprise. I asked him, "If you could replay that scene today with the knowledge you've gained in this class, what would you do differently?" He replied with confidence.

"First, I would recognize your father's sign for 'Deaf.' Then I would sign to both of the victims, 'Don't worry, I called an ambulance.' When the ambulance arrived, I would tell the emergency technician (EMT) that the victims were Deaf. Then, I would go after the driver and take his statement. But, this time, I would call for an interpreter to meet me at the hospital where I would interview your folks and write their account of the accident on my report, too."

The group cheered, and the deputy said to me, "I apologize for my ignorance at the time."

"Apology accepted," I assured him. "Let's forget the past and focus on the future."

It was gratifying to have enlightened the very officer who was at the scene of my parents' accident after so many years had passed...

My next stop was the Margate fire station. When I arrived, I found a motivated group of firefighters and EMTs awaiting me. They said they had never met a Deaf person, but were eager to prepare. I reviewed the ADA, taught some useful signs, and led practice on gestures and facial expressions that convey questions or give assurance. They were enthusiastic and determined learners.

When I arrived at my office the next day, I found a message on my answering machine from the captain at the firehouse. "Ruth," he said with glee, "we had our first Deaf patient last night, and it was thrilling!"

"We understood him, and he understood us. What a coincidence that you prepared us in time! Thank you." I imagined Mother and Dad smiling...

It was a lovely Friday, and there had been no walk-in clients for hours. I was thinking I might go home early when I heard a voice at the front desk, and our receptionist came to announce that Mr. Fischer, president of the Florida Association of the Deaf (FAD), wanted to meet with me.

His speech was excellent as he spoke his request. "Ruth, I tried to reserve a local hotel for a national conference of Deaf seniors, but the manager turned me down. I hope you can convince him to change his mind." I said, *"I'm interested, tell me more."*

He continued. "When I told him we will need closed captioning on the television broadcasts and TDDs with the room phones, he wrote back, 'Sorry, we are unable to accommodate your group.'" He put a card having the hotel's contact information on my desk.

"Please see what you can do, Ruth, a great many of us will be counting on you."

"I'll try my best, but I can't promise anything. I'll keep you posted." We shook hands, and he left.

On Monday morning, I wrote a letter on our agency's letterhead and addressed it to the hotel's corporate office. Introducing myself and DSC as representing Mr. Fischer, an officer of the FAD, I explained how the local hotel manager did not follow the Americans with Disabilities Act of 1990. I added, "Rather than take legal steps, Mr. Fischer requests that you inform

212

this manager of his responsibilities under the ADA and direct him to meet with Mr. Fischer again to contract for the conference." I signed the letter with my title, "Assistant to the Director." Those words should motivate action.

They did! I received a response from the local hotel manager the following week. He apologized for his error and invited Mr. Fischer to meet with him again. I accompanied Mr. Fischer to that meeting in a dual role: interpreter and consultant. Once the contract was signed, I enlisted Gallaudet University to install the needed equipment, leaving just one task for me: to recruit interpreters for the various Hearing presenters.

It was two weeks before the conference, interpreters were scheduled, and everything was arranged when I received a phone call from the local hotel manager with an unusual request.

"Can you come and teach my staff some signs to use during the event? There are three groups: food servers, front desk clerks, and housekeepers."

Teaching? He need say no more. This promised to be enjoyable, so I happily agreed to do the job.

I reported to the hotel a week before the event was to begin, and my three lists of signs were ready, each list suited to the appropriate group. The man at the desk led me to a large room set up with rows of chairs and then left to announce my arrival.

Soon the food servers came in, took seats, and we got to business. I said a word, showed its sign, and they copied my movement: *"coffee," "decaf," "water,"* "*sugar,*" etc. They excitedly took turns at role-playing as guests and servers, correcting each other.

The front desk clerks were next, and I again said each relevant term and showed the sign: "*dollars,*" "*pay,*" "*credit card,*" etc. They were enthusiastic, and they suggested more signs for me to teach them.

Last came the housekeepers. The supervisor who led them cautioned me. "These people are Haitian, and they don't speak English." I was stunned! I faced a language barrier. Talking to these folks would be like speaking to Deaf people who can't read lips.

Hmmm. Deaf people? Those words gave me an idea!

I taught silently using ASL signs and movements. For example, I pantomimed holding something big and wide, squeezing its softness, and placing it on my cheek while closing my eyes. Then I went to the nearby supply cabinet and selected a pillow. My students made the connection immediately. Next, I acted as if I were drinking from a glass and selected a drinking glass from the cabinet. All eyes sparkled with recognition when I introduced each term in a way I thought a Deaf guest would sign it. Finally, I tested each student in turn, and, every time a worker brought the correct article to me, the group clapped enthusiastically with delight.

As I drove home at the day's end, I felt it had been a productive and enjoyable experience for everyone.

The next morning I got a phone call from the hotel manager. He chuckled and said, "The Haitians were so delighted with your instruction that they now refer to you as 'teacher.' They want you to come back and teach them English. I had quite a time explaining that you couldn't do so." We both laughed, and I thanked him for the feedback.

The Haitians wanted to overcome their own language barrier, and their request touched my heart. I wished I had time to teach them.

Reportedly, this conference with a signing hotel staff was a smash hit, and the Deaf attendees raved about the unique experience. Some time later, Mr. Fischer came to my office and presented me with the NAD "Golden Hand" award and thanked me for my services. I laughed and told him, "I should thank YOU for allowing me to have such an interesting experience..."

I always enjoyed interpreting at weddings, they were easy and delightful routines. This wedding, however, was anything but routine to begin with, and it ended up as a unique experience, one that is permanently seared in my memory.

First, both the bride and groom were Deaf, and Bob and Dawn were invited guests. Arriving early, they chose the seats in the front row on my side of the platform to clearly view the couple and to watch my interpreting.

Then, this wedding was different in another way, for the ceremony was to be conducted jointly by a Jewish rabbi and a Catholic priest. Most of the guests were Deaf, and a few were Hearing relatives.

I stood beside the priest, facing the bride and groom. As he conducted his part of the ceremony, the couple's eyes were on me as I interpreted his statements. When the priest asked questions, first the bride, then the groom answered by signing and through my voice.

The priest sat down, and the rabbi took his place beside me, both of us facing the couple. Speaking to the groom, the rabbi asked, "Would you like to repeat your vows in Hebrew?"

When his question entered my ears and came out in my signing hands and fingers, I was stunned. I don't know Hebrew and definitely can't interpret it!

I glanced in panic at Bob and Dawn. In alarm, their eyes were as big as saucers. That didn't help a bit.

I struggled to keep calm and think quickly. Phonics! My kindergarten students used it to pronounce new words. If the groom replies yes, I will fingerspell the Hebrew syllables as they sound to me and silently form them on my lips as the rabbi says them. Hopefully, the groom can read lips.

I fixed my eyes on the groom and braced myself for his answer. He smiled and nodded yes. I took a deep breath as the rabbi began speaking the vows in Hebrew, pausing for the groom to repeat each phrase. As I fingerspelled the phonetic sounds and formed them on my lips, the rabbi's words started coming out of the groom's mouth! Amazingly, this process continued until the vows were completed. I stood amazed!

This seemed unreal until I heard Bob and Dawn sigh with relief and Hearing relatives murmur in surprise and delight.

Believe me, their relief, surprise, and delight were no greater than my own...

At a social gathering, I met a Hearing woman and her adult Deaf son, Kevin. As we chatted briefly, she told me she could not sign, and Kevin's speech was difficult for her to understand. It was obvious their communication was limited.

Not long after our meeting, she came to speak with me. "My son is in jail," she said, "please, will you help us?" and she told me what happened as she best understood it.

"Kevin was in a restaurant with a new buddy, a Hearing fellow who knew no sign, but Kevin got along with him by gesturing. They placed their order and were waiting for their food when the friend started banging on the table. The cafe owner called the police."

"The police arrived, and the Hearing friend spoke to them, pointing to Kevin. When the officers spoke to Kevin, he pointed to his ears and shook his head no to indicate he is Deaf and then he made the sign for 'Deaf', so the policemen used a common gesture similar to thumbing a ride to order him outside. Kevin was puzzled, so he used their gesture and asked, 'Why out? Why out?' in his garbled way."

"The policemen must have thought Kevin was threatening them because they grabbed him. When he resisted, they wrestled him outside, threw him on the sidewalk, and beat him up. Then they hauled him off to jail. He has a rib fracture and a head injury." Her tears flowed. "Kevin insists that he did nothing wrong and is innocent," she said, "but I want him to plead 'no contest.' In that way, he will accept the punishment, and the case will be over."

"But, if Kevin pleads 'not guilty,' he will go to trial, he'll lose, and he will be jail for a long time. Deaf people don't have a chance in court. Besides, he can't win a case against policemen! Will you please help me convince Kevin to plead 'no contest' and put himself at the judge's mercy?"

"Why don't you discuss this with Kevin and tell him what you told me?" I suggested. "It's not my place to persuade him of anything." She thought for a brief moment, then asked, "Would you please interpret when I speak with him? It's difficult for us to understand each other."

I explained that, in order to use my interpreting services, she needed to call the office and arrange it with the receptionist. She did so the following day.

We three met, and, after I interpreted his mother's argument, Kevin refused her advice. I voiced as he signed, "I am innocent, and that's the truth. I'll plead 'not guilty,' and take my chances with a jury." Turning on his heel, he marched out of the office, leaving his mother frantic. Before she followed, she said, "Ruth, I hope you will interpret at the trial."

A few days later, we received a call from a lawyer. Kevin requested that I interpret at his trial, so I was hired. While I had interpreted in jury rooms, I never interpreted a complete trial. Without a doubt, this would be a growing experience.

On the day of the trial, I interpreted the proceedings for Kevin as he sat with his mother in the front row of the courtroom. When he was called to testify, he sat in the witness chair beside the judge, and I faced both of them. Behind me stood the questioning lawyers, by turn, while the jury members sat to my left.

The trial lasted all morning, and, when we returned after lunch, the lawyers completed their cases. Kevin's lawyer gave his closing statements. "These policemen were not trained properly, so they did not understand the right of a Deaf person to have a sign language interpreter in that situation. Your honor and members of the jury, Kevin's civil rights were violated; the officers did not follow the federal ADA."

The jury filed out, and, in an hour, they brought the verdict: INNOCENT!

Kevin exclaimed in victory as his mother ran to embrace him. While they were distracted, I slipped out of the courtroom and walked to my car, my hands and arms aching from such a lengthy assignment. While I knew that sign language interpreters often got carpal tunnel syndrome, I considered this result worth the discomfort! ("Team interpreting" had not yet become the norm for such tasks.)

As I drove home, I was filled with joy at having played a part in a Deaf man's winning of justice. Perhaps Bob and I would go out to dinner to celebrate...

One evening Bob handed me an envelope that arrived in the day's mail. The return address showed it was from the RID. What in the world could this be about? I opened it to read that a fellow-interpreter filed a complaint in which she claimed I violated the RID Code of Ethics. A letter of support from her agency was enclosed.

This meant that, in order to keep my certification, I was to prove her claims wrong, and my response to the RID was due by a certain date. I tried to ignore rising fear and to stay calm.

As I read further, I recalled the event in question. Months earlier, I showed up for an interpreting assignment at a local business owned by Mr. and Mrs. Carr. When I walked in, Mrs. Carr met me.

"May I help you?"

"I'm the interpreter you hired from DSC last month. My name is Ruth Reppert, here is my business card."

"Then WHO is the interpreter in the next room?"

"I really don't know."

Mr. Carr appeared, and his wife asked the same question. He replied, "That lady is the interpreter I hired last week from the local Deaf services agency."

Realizing there was a mix-up, I assured them, "No problem, I will leave, and there will be no charge from DSC." But Mrs. Carr was determined as she yelled "NO!" to me and barked at her husband.

"I arranged for this interpreter with DSC a month ago, Michael, so the interpreter YOU hired from the other agency last week GOES, MINE STAYS!"

She firmly ordered me to follow her, and I complied, for it was she who had hired me for the job.

Mrs. Carr led me into a classroom where people sat in rows of chairs, waiting to see a video on a screen up front. I followed until she stopped beside two women sitting at the end of an aisle. I knew both the client and the interpreter.

Mrs. Carr pointed at her and sternly ordered, "Please leave! Ruth, here, will be our interpreter," and, as I signed her words for the Deaf client, I wished I were somewhere else. I felt awful for the woman who was ordered away, but I was caught in a tangled web of unfortunate circumstances.

The interpreter glared as she walked past me and mumbled, "This isn't the last you'll hear from me." This complaint to the RID obviously fulfilled her promise. She stated that I convinced the Carrs to dismiss her in favor of my services. I understood her conclusion, but it was based on incomplete and circumstantial evidence, and it was untrue.

I'll never forget the time I spent on my defense. The Carrs each wrote a letter testifying to the truth of my account, and, as I gathered more evidence to contradict my accuser's claims, Bob pointed out, "This is like the time you failed your RID test!"

Yes, politics had reared its ugly head again.

Thankfully, after reviewing my documents, the RID dismissed the case.

When I read that decision, I thought of how proud Mother and Celia would be of this fine organization they helped to establish. The RID safeguards Deaf clients, ensuring that they will receive accurate interpreting with ethical behavior from its tested and certified sign language interpreters.

Chapter 9

WINDUP

It was 1996! Where did the time go? Since retiring from teaching, I spent eleven years assisting Deaf and Hearing people. Lately, I was so busy, I seldom was at home. I knew I was neglecting my family, but I found it difficult to turn down an interpreting job. I just couldn't bring myself to say no when a Deaf person asked for my service.

Bob saved the day by suggesting we move, claiming it was the only way for me to get some rest. Toni supported his stance, so I gave in and agreed to move.

We three drove north, searching for a suitable home, and we found one in Vero Beach, Florida, a small sleepy town. As far as we knew, there were no Deaf people here and no agency serving the Deaf, so I could easily slow my pace.

About a month after we settled, Dawn invited us to Broward County saying that some of our friends wanted to have a little farewell party for us. When we arrived at the address, we found it was a huge church, and a large crowd waited there to greet us. They were the people, Hearing and Deaf, whose paths crossed ours: interpreters, sign language students, Deaf clients, and friends. Dawn had planned it all and was the hostess of the event.

Bob and I sat in wonder as people took turns on the platform, testifying about the ways he and I had influenced their lives, and we were overwhelmed by their gracious comments. For once, my ready hands were still; professional sign language interpreters provided their services.

As we watched and listened, I marveled at how a small gesture or service that I long ago forgot impacted another's life, and I whispered to Bob, "May I please use your handkerchief?" My tears needed dabbing.

When the program ended, Dawn invited me to give some final remarks. I mounted the platform with Bob at my side, looked out on the crowd, and with emotion welling up, I signed an impromptu speech, straight from my heart.

"Dear friends, thank you for this wonderful tribute. I am grateful to have shared life with you, but now we go our separate ways. As the days and years pass, the memory of our times here will fade. But, if anyone ever asks, 'Who is Ruth Reppert?' please tell them, 'She is a Hearing daughter of Deaf parents who loves us and worked hard for us.'"

As Bob and I descended the platform, John, a Deaf friend, sprang to his feet, and, facing the audience, he signed, *"Wait! There's one more person to honor: Bob! Ruth never could have accomplished so much without his support."* I squeezed Bob's hand in agreement as John led everyone in a hand-waving tribute to Bob.

It is a memory to treasure forever...

On the Platform

Bob, Toni, and I settled in Vero Beach and started a new life journey in an absolute paradise. We walked the beach as the waves of the Atlantic Ocean lapped at our feet, enjoyed the lush tropical growth of nearby McKee Botanical Garden, and boated on the Indian River Lagoon. We lunched at our favorite restaurant, the Lobster Shanty, while we watched dolphins at play.

I finally let go of the driving force that consumed me in Broward County. Here, in Indian River County, there would be no more association with deafness for us—or so we thought. We had no idea this was just a temporary lull. One phone call changed our plans.

I answered, and a man calling from Gospel Publishing House (GPH) introduced himself.

"Ruth, because you grew up with Deaf parents and have broad teaching experience, Ed Lawrence suggested that you are best qualified to write a teacher's guide for his book, 'Sign Language Made Simple.' Are you willing to tackle the project? It will be a great help for teachers who use the book in classroom settings."

My thoughts raced. A teacher's guide will equip both Deaf and Hearing signers to teach Contact Signing, and more Hearing folks will learn to sign with Deaf people. On the other hand, I've never written a book. It would be a growing experience.

I replied, "I'll think about it and get back to you." I discussed it with Bob, and, as usual, he encouraged me, so I called GPH and accepted the challenge.

For the next three years, I spent every spare minute in my little home office, immersed in a new project. It was hard work, but I finally completed the "Instructor's Guide for Sign Language Made Simple," published by GPH in 1999.

During the period I was writing, an event caught my eye. Bob and I were standing at the service counter of the Modern Age furniture store in a section of Vero Beach called "Miracle Mile" when we overheard the clerk behind the counter speaking loudly with exaggerated speech. I turned to see a young man writing on a notepad, and the two were exchanging notes. I was sure the man was Deaf.

I looked at Bob pleadingly, and he smiled, so I waved discreetly at the man, caught his attention, and asked, "*Are you Deaf?*" He perked up and answered, "*Yes! Can you please help us?*" and a few minutes of my interpreting settled their matter. That was all I needed. This little frog hopped right back into the Deaf World.

Bob laughed and said, "This shopping area is aptly named, 'Miracle Mile!'"

Before we knew it, Bob and I were involved with the nearest service agency, Deaf and Hard of Hearing Services of the Treasure Coast (DHHS), located in Jensen Beach. The director, Rick Kottler, was trying to expand his agency's services to Deaf and hard of hearing people in Vero Beach, and Bob and I wanted to help. We explored and found a church in town willing to provide a rent-free office for DHHS.

Soon I was teaching classes in Contact Signing at the new office and accepting interpreting assignments from Rick. I interpreted at the courthouse in Vero Beach, in classes at Indian River Community College, and at the Okeechobee courthouse, to name a few. I also worked with the public school interpreters in St. Lucie County to expand their interpreting skills. My assignments were not as frequent as they had been in Broward County.

One day Rick asked me to go with him to a United Way board meeting in downtown Vero Beach to seek funding for DHHS. He said, "I'd like you to share some of your insights as a child of Deaf parents. I hope we can open eyes to the need."

I agreed to go. Rick and I spoke to a group of very attentive Hearing people on the importance of DHHS services to Deaf and hard of hearing folks, and, not long after that meeting, DHHS won United Way funding. Our mission was accomplished.

These activities pleased me, and I assured Bob I would keep my "Deaf projects" to a minimum. He grinned and signed Dad's familiar comment, *"I know you through and through."* The truth is, he has affection and admiration for Deaf people, too. After living with me all these years, it came about naturally...

Life was calming down, and my energies were waning when I got a call from Deborah Borfitz, a writer for the Vero Beach Magazine, a local publication. She asked if I would be willing to interpret while she interviewed a young Deaf couple working at the Disney Vero Beach Resort. She wanted to include their story in an article she was writing. We had a nice chat, and I agreed to do the job. I met her and her subjects at the resort as planned, and all went smoothly.

When the magazine was published, I got a copy and enjoyed reading Deborah's article, "Learning to Live in a Silent World—Breaking the Sound Barrier." She had researched her subject in depth, interviewing interpreters, Deaf adults, and local Deaf children and their parents. Her article was thorough, bringing the readers current on local happenings in the field of deafness. As I read her commentary, I realized: Vero Beach isn't sleepy anymore! I treasure the January 2003 issue of the Vero Beach Magazine. We proudly display it on our coffee table...

Dad often said, "Time flies," and I have seen it whizz by, bringing an enormous amount of change, some of it observed on Google Earth.

Our shack on Perchment Street is leveled, and the stairway to Frankstown Avenue is completely hidden by overgrowth.

The Frankstown Avenue homes remain intact, but they show their age.

Gramma's row house on Conemaugh Street is still there, but all the houses show the ravages of time, and the field across the street is now a gas station.

Crescent Elementary School stands as I remember it, and it is still a functioning school with a Website.

Blackadore Avenue Presbyterian Church closed its doors in 1990. There is no trace of it.

The row of houses on Durango Way has been razed.

Baxter Junior High School is still in use and was listed on the National Register of Historic Places in 1986.

The programs I started in Broward County have ceased. No doubt advanced technology and improved awareness made them no longer useful.

DSC closed in 1998 due to lack of funding.

Toni's cancer returned in 2001. When her doctor revealed Dr. Bryant's prediction, she thanked us for not telling her. This time Toni lost the battle. As she lay dying, we held hands and thanked God for her ten added years of life.

My instructor's guide was discontinued in 2013, but the fourteen years of robust sales indicate that many instructors taught continuing education classes where Hearing folks learned to talk with Deaf people using Contact Signing and befriended a few along the way.

If Mother and Dad and their friends were alive today, they would be amazed at the progress, much of it due to technology. Growing awareness of the Deaf community and the public's keen interest in signing would please them.

I still hear Dad telling me to teach Hearing people about the Deaf and to teach them basic sign communication. So, while I no longer visit any Club of the Deaf nor interpret on call, I am at my computer, marketing "Sign Language Made Simple" and its practice DVD at <u>www.signlanguagemadesimple.com.</u>

Ruth and Bob, Retirees

CONCLUSION

U ncle Dan was right! Mother and Dad needed me as a connection to the Hearing World, but he had no way of knowing that their Deaf friends would need me, too.

I welcomed my role as family interpreter, but I felt pressured when my parents expected me to interpret for others. I believe my parents intended no harm in this. Besides, those stressful times gave me insights, abilities, and strengths I might not have gained otherwise. Maria Montessori's claim rings true for me; my early experiences influenced my life. And I realize that everything worked together for good, just as Romans 8:28 declares.

The Deaf people I have known accepted their deafness without shame, anger, or self-pity and lived productive lives, working diligently for the Deaf community to improve their lot and to eliminate the injustices of the Hearing World. They challenged those wrongs with patience, respectful debate, and education, and sign language interpreters were vital to their progress.

I am privileged to be the daughter of Edwin and Irene and to be Half-Hearing and Half-Deaf. And I am blessed to be the wife of Bob Reppert, a more supportive husband surely cannot exist. As the 1982 song says, he is "the wind beneath my wings."

AFTERWORD

Helen Keller once said, "The world is moved along, not only by the mighty shoves of its heroes, but also by the aggregate of the tiny pushes of each honest worker."

My heroes were visionaries. With their mighty shoves, they inspired my tiny pushes, and I gratefully honor each of them here.

They leave an inspiring legacy.

Edwin M. Hazel, 1894-1983, who did his utmost to teach his Deaf peers how to hold productive meetings in their struggle for civil rights. His parliamentary law chart and slide rule placed quick answers at their fingertips, and his question-and-answer columns equipped them further.

Irene S. Hazel, 1908-1988, who served the Deaf community through local Clubs and the National Fraternal Society of the Deaf and taught signing and interpreting to Hearing folks. In 1964, she met with a group, Hearing and Deaf, at Ball State University to establish the Registry of Interpreters for the Deaf.

Dr. Thomas A. Mayes, 1920-1999, a pioneer of continuing education programs for Hearing and Deaf adults and their deaf children, who became Gallaudet University's first Deaf vice president in continuing education and advocacy in 1941 and is hailed by the Deaf community as "Father of Continuing Education."

<u>Julia Burg Mayes</u>, 1921-2003, who taught Deaf students for over thirty-seven years, first at the Michigan School for the Deaf and then at the Model Secondary School for the Deaf at Gallaudet University.

<u>Dr. Frank B. Sullivan,</u> 1923-2003, who led the National Fraternal Society of the Deaf to become a multi-million dollar entity, helped the Deaf keep the right to drive, and promoted their access to television through closed captioning.

<u>Celia Burg Warshawsky,</u> 1921-1986, an activist with the Chicago Hearing Society, who debated before federal, state, city, and private agencies to win Illinois legislation providing TDDs to Deaf people.

<u>Leonard Warshawsky,</u> 1920-1994, faithful Grand Secretary of the National Fraternal Society of the Deaf for more than thirty years.

My Role Models
Lenny, Irene, Celia, Edwin, Tom, Julia

A DICTIONARY GAME
Using the World Wide Web

Search the term. Read about it. Define it in a sentence.

American Manual Alphabet

American Sign Language

Americans with Disabilities Act

Closed Captioning

CODA International

Contact Signing

Deaf American (magazine)

Gallaudet University

National Association of the Deaf

Parliamentary Law

Qualified Interpreter

Quality Assurance Tests

Registry of Interpreters for the Deaf

Sign Language Interpreting

Silent Worker (magazine)

State Associations of the Deaf

State Schools for the Deaf

Telecommunication Device for the Deaf

Telecommunications Relay Service

Video Relay Services

Video Remote Interpreting

Printed in the USA
CPSIA information can be obtained
at www.ICGtesting.com
LVHW020818200823
755497LV00012B/398